My Weird

Jokes, Games, and Puzzles

Dan Gutman

Pictures by
Jim Paillot

HARPER

An Imprint of HarperCollinsPublishers

TO NINA

The author gratefully acknowledges
the editorial contributions of Nina Wallace.

My Weird School: Jokes, Games, and Puzzles
Text copyright © 2018 by Dan Gutman
Illustrations copyright © 2018 by Jim Paillot

ISBN 978-0-06-279687-5

Typography by Laura Mock
18 19 20 21 22   CG/BRR   10 9 8 7 6 5 4 3 2 1
❖
First Edition

CONTENTS

---

*In case you were wondering, it's all about My Weird School.

INTRODUCTION

My name is A.J. and you know what? I hate puzzles.

Puzzles are no fun at all. You want to know why? Because puzzles force you to think. And thinking is hard! One time, I thought so hard that I thought my head was going to explode.*

I'd just like to say that my name is Andrea and I *love* puzzles!

Oh no! It's Andrea Young, this annoying girl in my class with curly brown hair! Who let *you* in here?

Arlo, you know perfectly well that you and I were assigned to write this *together.* It's part of our project for the gifted and

---

*What are you looking down here for?

talented program, remember?

Shhhhh! Don't tell everybody I'm in the gifted and talented program! That's a program for nerds, like you.

The truth is that puzzles are fun, and they're *good* for kids. They're sort of like vegetables and I *love* vegetables. Puzzles make you smarter, because they stimulate your brain.*

Ugh, gross! Disgusting! I don't want my brain stimulated. I'd rather play video games.

Video games *are* puzzles, Arlo! They're just puzzles that are on a screen instead of on a page.

Oh. I knew that. Okay, never mind all that stuff I said about puzzles.

---

*I can't believe you looked down here *again*. Man, you'll fall for *anything*!

There are a bunch of puzzles in this book. Find a word. Crosswords. Mazes. Every kind of puzzle you can think of. And there are a bunch of games and jokes in here too.

So we hope you enjoy them. I just hope your head doesn't explode. That would hurt.*

Yours truly,

Professor A.J., the Professor of Puzzles

Andrea Young, the Princess of Puzzles

---

*Okay, that's it. I'm not telling you again. Stop looking down here!

PART 1

WHO TEACHES WHAT?

Directions: Do you think you know everything there is to know about Ella Mentry School? Match the teacher with what he or she teaches.

MISS DAISY_____

MISS HOLLY_____

MR. MACKY_____

MS. HANNAH _____

MISS SMALL _____

MR. HYNDE _____

MRS. YONKERS _____

MR. DOCKER _____

second grade Spanish reading art
gym music science computer skills

2

ART SUPPLY SCRAMBLE

Directions: Unscramble the letters below to find out what Ms. Hannah keeps in her art supply closet.

1. RIFNEG TINAP_____

2. LEGU TISSCK_____

3. TERGTIL _____

4. BRADACORD _____

5. SISCROSS _____

6. SPANESPREW _____

7. ACORNSY_____

8. STRIPNASHBUE _____

FIZZ ED!

Directions: Miss Small is off the wall! Use this secret code to swap in letters below and find out what crazy things Miss Small has the kids do in fizz ed.

A B C D E F G H I J K L M
Z N E B H R K A U I F C W

N O P Q R S T U V W X Y Z
O L J D Q V P Y X G S M T

P I W W O C   X L H F S C X

D H O H B L C   K C H Z E C F X

L E J L G C B   Q H B L C

Bonus: What is Miss Small's motto?

K I B ′ K I B ′ K I B

H O O Z E C   Z J Y C !

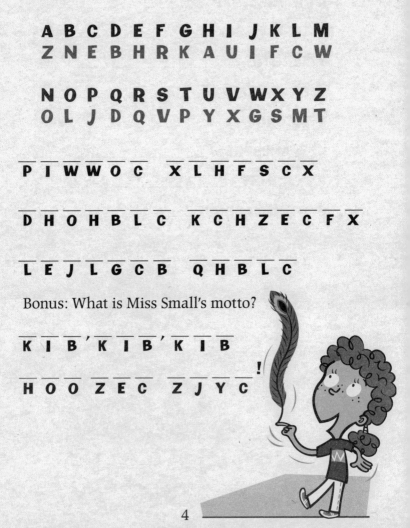

A.J.'S SUDOKU FUN

Directions: Help A.J. solve this tricky math puzzle. Fill in all the boxes using only the numbers 1 to 4. Each row and column and each group of four boxes inside the thicker lines must contain each number only once.

	3		4
2			
			3
3			

2 + 2 = 4

2 × 2 = 4

CHOCOLATE PARTY
WORD SEARCH

Directions: To celebrate finishing one million math problems, Ella Mentry School is having a chocolate party! Yum! There are ten kinds of chocolate candies hiding in the jumble of letters below. Can you find them all?

```
Z S V E Y P O P H T B F A J Y
A N R D O L T A M O U R T M N
W I C L E S V X N O T Z P I R
L C P A T I U F Y T T O B L Z
G K M I L K D U D S E V R K T
R E G G Q I H A R I R T A Y Z
A R L E G T C A S E F F T W E
P S B O N K T R A R I P L A N
L E M A G A R A I O N N B Y S
A D N F L T G E N L G A D P T
M O U N D S D G H L E Q S V X
C U F J A P B A B Y R U T H O
T A H E R S H E Y B A R T I L
B O N M J D F K S U D B O Y T
O J U N I O R M I N T S K A P
```

**Snickers Kit Kat Milk Duds Milky Way
Junior Mints Baby Ruth Hershey Bar
Mounds Tootsie Roll Butterfinger**

6

MISS DAISY IS CRAZY!

Directions: Miss Daisy says she forgot how to do these math problems. Can you help her solve them?

8 + 6 = _____

7 + 5 = _____

41 + 9 = _____

5 + 74 = _____

65 + 3 + 7 = _____

38 + 2 + 2 = _____

52 + 3 – 9 = _____

9 + 28 – 3 = _____

TEACHERS IN LOVE

Directions: Miss Daisy and Mr. Macky are getting married, and the whole school is invited! Help the bride and groom navigate this maze so they're not late to their own wedding.

NURSERY RHYME WEEK

Directions: It's Nursery Rhyme Week at Ella Mentry School! Mrs. Roopy sat on a wall and had a great fall. Help put her together again by completing the nursery rhyme titles below.

1. JACK AND _____

2. LITTLE MISS _____

3. HUMPTY _____

4. _____ BO PEEP

5. WEE _____ WINKIE

6. _____ PORGIE

7. PETER PETER _____ EATER

8. _____ SIMON

RAPPIN' AND RHYMIN' WITH MR. HYNDE

Directions: Mr. Hynde is the music teacher at Ella Mentry School. He's also out of his mind, and he loves to rap! Help him finish his latest rap song by filling in the blanks.

WHEN I'M RAPPIN' I NEED A BEAT.
AND WHEN I'M HUNGRY, I LIKE TO_____.

WHEN I'M THIRSTY, I TAKE A DRINK.
THEN I WASH THE DISHES IN THE_____.

WHEN I'M DOWN, I'M FEELING BLUE.
PIGS WILL SQUEAL AND COWS WILL_____.

SOME DAYS WHEN I'M NOT IN SCHOOL,
I GO SWIMMING IN A_____.

TO FEED MY BRAIN, I READ A BOOK.
TO FEED MY BELLY, I LIKE TO_____.

TO MAKE AN EGG, I ALWAYS BOIL IT.
WHEN I GOTTA GO, I USE THE_____.

WHEN I'M TIRED, I TAKE A NAP.
BUT MOSTLY I JUST LIKE TO_____.

WHO'S WHO?

Directions: Match the names with what the teachers do at Ella Mentry School.

MR. KLUTZ _____

MRS. ROOPY _____

MRS. COONEY _____

MS. LAGRANGE _____

MISS LAZAR _____

MRS. KORMEL _____

MRS. PATTY _____

MR. MACKY _____

MR. LOUIE _____

crossing guard bus driver school nurse
principal secretary reading specialist
custodian librarian lunch lady

SAY GOOD-BYE TO SUGAR!

Directions: Oh no! Mrs. Cooney is banning junk food from the cafeteria! Unscramble the following letters to find some healthy snacks for A.J.

1. ESECHE KISTC _____

2. RANISIS _____

3. NOGEAR _____

4. PLEAP _____

5. GROUTY _____

6. ARGEPS _____

7. ROTSCAR _____

8. TUNAPES _____

MUSICAL MAYHEM CROSSWORD

Directions: Answer the clues to fill in the blanks and find out all about music class at Ella Mentry School.

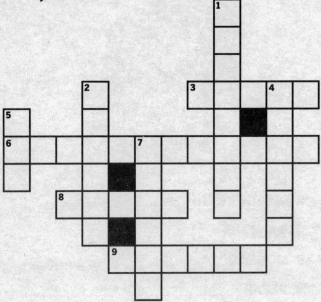

Across

3. Mr. Hynde plays Mr. Klutz's head like a _____.

6. Name of show Mr. Hynde is on.

8. Mr. Hynde spins on his head on the _____.

9. Andrea takes lessons in this instrument.

Down

1. Music teacher before Mr. Hynde.
2. Color of Mr. Hynde's cape.
4. Mr. Hynde is a One-Man Funky _____ Machine.
5. Kind of music Mr. Hynde sings.
7. Mr. Loring's favorite song is "Who Put the _____ in the Cookie Jar?"

SPORTS SEARCH

Directions: Find twelve sports A.J., Michael, Neil, and Ryan love to play in the jumble of letters below.

```
W B V E Y P O P H T B T V F X
R S K A T E B O A R D I N G N
E I I L E S A X N O I T P Z R
S C C I L K S U D V R T B L Z
T K K A T I E F Y S T E R F T
L E B G Q T B A R I B R A Y Z
I R A E F K A A S E I F T W E
N S L B O W L I N G K P L A N
G E L A O T L A I T E N N I S
A D N F T A G E N L S A D P O
F R I S B E E G H L E Q S V C
C U F J A P B A H O C K E Y C
T A H E L S H E Y B A R T I E
B O N M L D F K S U D B O Y R
W M I N I A T U R E G O L F P
```

Frisbee football skateboarding hockey
dirt bikes wrestling kickball tennis
baseball bowling soccer miniature golf

16

THROWING UP ON THE ROOF!

Directions: Unscramble the letters below to find out what stuff Miss Lazar finds on the school roof.

1. LULERAMB _____

2. FLABTOOL _____

3. ALEBLABS PAC _____

4. BONETOKO _____

5. OYYO _____

6. SIRBEEF _____

7. ENSNIT CRETAK _____

FUN WITH POTATOES!

Directions: Mr. Docker is obsessed with potatoes! Complete the answers below using only the letters in:

POTATO CLOCK

1. A POPULAR MEXICAN FOOD _____

2. A TYPE OF LARGE PARROT _____

3. CHOCOLATY HOT DRINK _____

4. A LIVELY TYPE OF DANCE _____

5. A POPULAR SODA FLAVOR _____

6. ANOTHER WORD FOR "CAPE" _____

7. TO APPLAUD _____

8. COMPLETE OR ABSOLUTE _____

MRS. KORMEL IS NOT NORMAL!

Directions: Mrs. Kormel, the school bus driver, invents her own secret language. Match her words to their meanings below.

1. BINGLE BOO _____

2. LIMPUS KIDOODLE _____

3. ZINGY ZIP_____

4. BIX BLATTINGER _____

5. PINKLE BURFLE NOBIN _____

Quiet down   curse word   Sit down
Get off the bus   Hello

MASHED POTATO MESSAGE

Directions: The lunch lady—Ms. LaGrange—is strange! She writes a secret message in the mashed potatoes—YAWYE. Use this secret code below to swap in letters and find out what it means.

A	B	C	D	E	F	G	H	I	J	K	L	M
Z	N	E	B	H	R	K	A	U	I	F	C	W

N	O	P	Q	R	S	T	U	V	W	X	Y	Z
O	L	J	D	Q	V	P	Y	X	G	S	M	T

U N I   H F C   M E H Z   U N I

C H Z

Bonus: What is Ms. LaGrange's catchphrase?

W J S C   T C H X   H

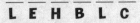

L E H B L C

PRESIDENTIAL TRUE OR FALSE

Directions: It's Presidents' Day, and Mr. Macky teaches A.J.'s class all about our presidents. Circle which presidential facts below are true and which are false. (Hint: You can find all the answers in *My Weird School #15: Mr. Macky Is Wacky!* Or, with help from your parents or a teacher, you can try looking up the answers online.)

1. Franklin Roosevelt's mother made him wear dresses until he was five. **T F**
2. Abraham Lincoln had wooden teeth. **T F**
3. Ulysses S. Grant smoked twenty cigars a day. **T F**
4. Andrew Johnson never went to school. **T F**
5. Thomas Jefferson grew some of the first tomatoes in America. **T F**
6. John Quincy Adams liked to go skinny-dipping. **T F**
7. Benjamin Franklin was our third president. **T F**

MS. TODD'S MATH JOKES

Ms. Todd is odd. She *loves* math! But she also tells these silly math jokes, so maybe she's not so bad after all.

WHY WAS THE MATH BOOK SAD?
It had too many problems.

WHY DID THE TWO 4S SKIP DINNER?
Because they already 8

WHAT DID THE TRIANGLE SAY TO THE CIRCLE?
You're pointless.

WHY WAS 6 AFRAID OF 7?
Because 7 8 9

WHAT DO YOU CALL MATH FRIENDS?
Algebros

WHAT DO YOU CALL A NUMBER THAT CAN'T KEEP STILL?
A roamin' numeral

HOW DO YOU MAKE SEVEN AN EVEN NUMBER?
Take the *s* out.

HOW DO YOU MAKE ONE VANISH?
Add a *g* and it's gone.

WHY WAS 8 NOT FRIENDS WITH 3?

Because 3 was odd

WHY DID THE BOY KEEP A RULER UNDER HIS PILLOW?

To see how long he could sleep

WHAT TOOL DO YOU USE FOR MATH?

MultiPLIERS

WHAT IS A MATH TEACHER'S FAVORITE SEASON?

SUMmer

DRAW AND COLOR
LIKE CRAZY!

Eeeek! All the color has gone out of A.J.'s face!
And his clothes! It's a catastrophe!* Quick, grab
some pencils or crayons before it's too late! Draw
A.J. in the empty box below. Then color in the
cover on the right. The fate of the world is in
your hands!

---

*That's when something horrible happens to a cat.

SPOT THE DIFFERENCES

Directions: These two covers are almost identical. But there are a few differences. Can you spot them? (Hint: There are six.)

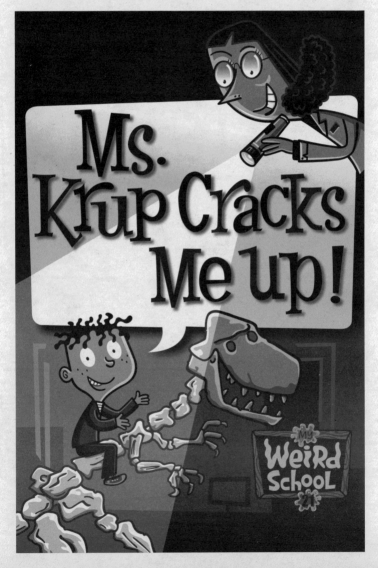

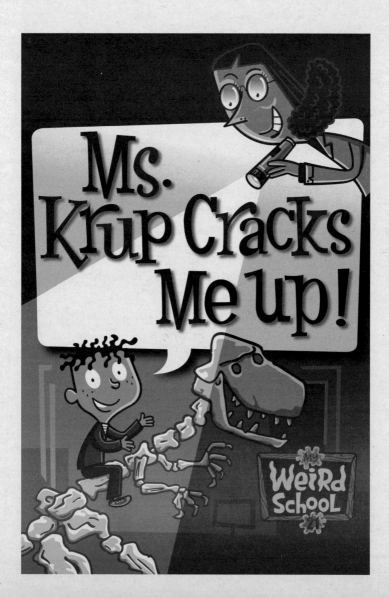

WACKY WORD STORY TIME

Directions: Before you read this story, fill in each blank with a word that fits the description next to it. After you fill in all the blanks, go back and read the story out loud. Is it funny? Or just really weird?

"My name is A.J. and I hate _____ (*plural noun*)."

Our teacher, Miss Daisy, was taking attendance. It was the first day of second grade. Miss Daisy told everyone in the class to stand up and say our name and something about_____ (*plural noun*).

All the kids laughed when I said I hated _____ (*plural noun*). But there was nothing funny about it. I have learned a lot in my _____ (*number*) years. One thing I learned is that there is no reason why a _____(*noun*) should have to _____ (*verb*) a _____ (*noun*).

If you ask me, kids can learn all we need to learn by watching TV. You can learn important information, like which _____ (*noun*) tastes best and what _____ (*noun*) you should buy, and which _____ (*noun*) leaves your hair the shiniest. This is stuff that we'll need to know when we grow up.

If you ask me, school is just this dumb thing that grown-ups thought up so they wouldn't have to pay for _____ (*plural noun*). When I grow up and have children of my own, I won't ever make them _____ (*verb*). They can just ride their _____ (*noun*) and play _____ (*game*) all day. They'll be happy, and they'll think I'm the greatest dad in the world.

But for now I wanted to let my new teacher, Miss Daisy, know from the very start how I felt about _____ (*plural noun*).

"You know what, A.J.?" Miss Daisy said. "I hate _____ (*same as previous word*) too."

"You do?"

We all stared at Miss Daisy. I thought teachers loved _____ (*same as previous word*). If they didn't love _____ (*same as previous word*), why did they become teachers? I know that when I'm a grown-up, I'm not going to go anywhere near _____ (*same as previous word*).

"Sure I hate _____ (*same as previous word*)," Miss Daisy continued. "If I didn't have to be here teaching you, I could be home sitting on my _____ (*noun*), watching TV, and eating _____ (*plural noun*)."

"Wow!" we all said.

"What are _____ (*same as previous word*)?" asked Ryan, a kid with black sneakers who was sitting next to me.

"_____ (*same as previous word*) are these wonderful chocolate _____ (*plural noun*)," Miss Daisy told us. "They're about the size of a large _____ (*noun*), and you can pop the whole thing right in your mouth so you don't need a _____ (*noun*). I could eat a whole box of _____ (*plural noun*) in one sitting."

"They sound delicious!" said Andrea Young, a girl with curly brown _____ (*noun*). She was sitting up real straight in the front of the class with her _____ (*plural noun*) folded like they were attached to each other.

Miss Daisy sounded like a pretty cool lady, for a teacher. Anybody who hated _____ (*plural noun*) and liked to sit around watching TV and eating chocolate _____ (*plural noun*) was okay by me.

Me and Miss Daisy had a lot in common. Maybe second grade wouldn't be so terrible after all.

MY WEIRD SCHOOL TRIVIA

There's no way in a million hundred years you'll get all these answers right. So nah-nah-nah boo-boo on you! (Hint: All the answers to the questions below come from the My Weird School series.)

Q: HOW MUCH DOES MR. KLUTZ CHARGE THE KIDS TO RENT THE SCHOOL FOR ONE NIGHT?

A: One million pages of reading

Q: WHAT DID MR. KLUTZ DO BEFORE HE BECAME A PRINCIPAL?

A: He was a physics teacher.

Q: WHAT DOES MRS. ROOPY HAVE ABOVE HER BELLY BUTTON?

A: A heart-shaped tattoo

Q: WHAT IS THE WORST WEEK OF THE YEAR FOR A.J. AND HIS FRIENDS?

A: TV Turnoff Week

Q: WHAT SONG DOES MR. HYNDE SING ON *AMERICAN IDOL*?

A: "Tomorrow" from *Annie*

Q: WHAT IS MRS. COONEY'S CURE FOR A.J.'S HEADACHE?

A: Balance a yardstick on his nose while hopping on one foot and clucking like a chicken

Q: WHAT DO THE INITIALS SC ON MISS LAZAR'S OVERALLS STAND FOR?

A: Super Custodian

Q: WHAT DOES M.E.A.N. STAND FOR?

A: Make Excellence a Necessity

Q: WHAT DOES MR. DOCKER CALL HIS POTATO-POWERED CAR?

A: The Spudmobile

Q: WHAT DOES A.J. CALL THE LOST AND FOUND?

A: The free stuff room

Q: WHAT DOES ANDREA GET A.J. FOR HIS SECRET SANTA PRESENT?

A: A hat

Q: WHO IS THE ONLY AUTHOR A.J. THINKS IS COOL?

A: Dr. Seuss

Q: WHO DO THE KIDS ELECT PRESIDENT OF ELLA MENTRY SCHOOL?

A: Mr. Wiggles, Neil the nude kid's pet ferret

Q: WHAT DOES A.J. TELL THE KINDERGARTEN CLASS ANDREA'S REAL NAME IS?

A: Underwear Face

Q: WHAT IS MR. KLUTZ'S WIFE'S NAME?

A: Karla Klutz

Q: WHAT DID MR. LOUIE DO BEFORE HE WAS A CROSSING GUARD?

A: He was a judge.

Q: WHAT IS THE NAME OF THE HISSING COCKROACH IN THE NATURAL HISTORY MUSEUM?

A: General Muffin

Q: WHAT IS THE NAME OF MRS. YONKERS'S TURTLE?

A: Speedy

Q: WHAT WAS IN MISS SUKI KABUKI'S MYSTERY BOX?

A: Rappy, a peregrine falcon

Q: WHAT IS MRS. YONKERS'S LATEST TOP SECRET INVENTION?

A: A remote control remote control

Q: HOW MANY TILES ARE THERE IN THE HALLWAY BETWEEN MISS DAISY'S CLASS AND DR. CARBLES'S OFFICE?

A: 4,324

Q: WHAT DOES A.J. GIVE MISS DAISY FOR A WEDDING PRESENT?

A: His old skateboard

PART 2

FUN IN THE SUN CROSSWORD

Directions: A.J.'s and Andrea's families share a beach house over the summer. What could possibly go wrong? Fill in the clues to reveal some beachy answers!

Across

3. This protects you from the sun's rays.

4. A bird you find at the beach

6. A kind of summer footwear

8. This person will save you from drowning.

9. Swimmers are afraid of these fish.

Down

1. Mr. Sunny is building this.

2. Something you collect on the beach

5. Summer temperature

7. The ocean makes lots of these.

HINKY PINKIES

Directions: Fill in the blanks based on the clues below. The answers to Hinky Pinkies are two rhyming words of two syllables each. To help you get the hang of it, we answered the first one for you. You're welcome!

1. GLOVE FOR A BABY CAT: <u>KITTEN MITTEN</u>

2. MISS DAISY'S BABY: _____

3. ROCKY CELESTIAL BODY: _____

4. BIZARRE FLOWER: _____

5. HAPPY CHRISTMAS SHRUB: _____

6. CHEERFUL JOKE: _____

7. COACH HYATT'S SON: _____

JAIL JUMBLE

Directions: Officer Spence makes no sense! And neither do these jumbled letters, but when you unscramble them, they're all words that mean "jail." Hopefully Officer Spence will get unscrambled and stop sending all the Ella Mentry School teachers there for no reason!

1. MARMLES _____

2. SOLOBEACA _____

3. ROOCLE _____

4. NKLCI _____

5. TINJO _____

6. KYPOE _____

7. OGOESWHO _____

TEAM SPIRIT CHEERS

Directions: Andrea and Emily are cheerleaders for A.J.'s Pee Wee football team! Complete their cheers using the list of words below.

tie shout great friends dirt
hate batter right

JUMP IN THE AIR! FALL IN THE _____ !
JUST MAKE SURE NO ONE GETS HURT!

LAUGH AND PLAY AND _____ AND SING!
WINNING ISN'T EVERYTHING!

LOSING! WINNING! WE WON'T LIE!
WE'RE MOST HAPPY WITH A _____ !

WE DON'T _____ AND WE DON'T BOO!
WE RESPECT THE OTHER TEAM, TOO!

FOOTBALL HAS A KICKER. BASEBALL HAS A
_____ !
WHATEVER GAME WE PLAY, THE SCORE
DOESN'T MATTER!

WINNING! LOSING! IT DEPENDS!

WHY CAN'T WE JUST ALL BE _____?

THAT'S ALL _____! THAT'S OKAY!

WE'RE GONNA WIN IT ANYWAY!

IT'S OKAY THAT WE'RE NOT _____!

AT LEAST WE ALL PARTICIPATE!

PERFECT FOOD COMBOS

Directions: A.J. and the gang love peanut butter and jelly sandwiches. They're the perfect combo! Match the foods below to their perfect combos.

PEANUT BUTTER AND JELLY
GO TOGETHER LIKE . . .

I. PEACHES AND _____

2. FISH AND _____

3. FRANKS AND _____

4. BACON AND _____

5. MACARONI AND _____

6. MILK AND _____

7. SPAGHETTI AND _____

8. PEAS AND _____

9. CHEESE AND _____

IO. BURGER AND _____

crackers eggs fries meatballs cream cheese
cookies beans carrots chips

42

TRUE OR FALSE?

Directions: Dr. Brad, the school counselor, has gone mad! He uses a lie detector to find out what's true and what's false. What will *you* use? Circle the correct answer.

1. Mrs. Lizzy is not a real teacher. **T F**
2. Mr. Granite is from the planet Uranus. **T F**
3. Ms. LaGrange is from Spain. **T F**
4. Mrs. Roopy's hero is Melvil Dewey. **T F**
5. There's a hot tub in the teachers' lounge. **T F**
6. A.J. loves Mrs. Cooney. **T F**
7. Miss Lazar loves when kids make messes. **T F**
8. Mrs. Dole is Ryan's mom. **T F**
9. Miss Mary is Mr. Klutz's daughter. **T F**
10. Ms. Leakey opened a McDonald's restaurant.
    T F

PRINCIPAL CAMP
WORD SEARCH

Directions: Mr. Klutz is going away to principal camp. Yippee! Will the principals toast marshmallows? Find ten activities they will do there.

```
Z S V P Y P O P H H B B A L Y
A N R I O L T A M P U U T A N
W I C N E S V X N A L P P N R
D O D G E B A L L R T T B Y Z
C A M P F I R E Y A E E R A T
R E G O Q T H A R C R Z F R T
A R L N G K C A S H F C T D E
A S B G N A T R A U I R L S N
R E M A G T R A I T N A B Y S
C A N O E I N G N I G F D P T
H B U N D S D G H N E T S V X
E U S W I M M I N G R S T H O
R A K D R S H E C R V W Q S L
Y O N R O C K C L I M B I N G
O H O M T W P P C L T S K A P
```

lanyards archery rock climbing parachuting
crafts swimming canoeing dodgeball
Ping Pong campfire

DR. BRAD'S DICTIONARY

Directions: Dr. Brad talks like a mad scientist! Match his words to their meaning below. (Hint: All the answers can be found in *My Weird School Daze #7: Dr. Brad Has Gone Mad!*)

ZEEZ _____

SHTOP _____

VERD _____

FURZER _____

UZZER _____

EES _____

ZINK _____

ANUZER _____

EET _____

VY _____

ZEND _____

VILL _____

VERLD _____

VEN _____

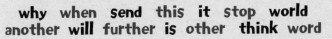

why when send this it stop world
another will further is other think word

45

BETCHA CAN'T SAY THIS THREE TIMES FAST!

Directions: The speech teacher, Miss Laney, is zany! See if you can say her tongue twisters below. Bonus: Try to say them out loud, three times fast!

I thought a thought. But the thought I thought wasn't the thought I thought I thought.

Chester cheetah chews a chunk of cheap chewy Cheddar cheese.

The two-toed tree toad tried to tread where the three-toed tree toad trod.

Does this shop sport short socks with spots?

While we were walking, we were watching window washers wash Washington's windows with warm washing water.

Did Doug dig Dick's garden or was Doug's garden the garden Dick dug?

Which wristwatches are Swiss wristwatches?

Lesser leather never weathered wetter weather better.

To begin to toboggan, don't buy too big a toboggan. Too big a toboggan is too big a toboggan to buy to begin to toboggan.

What time does the wristwatch strap shop shut?

Betty bought a bit of bitter butter that made her batter bitter, but Betty bought a bit of better butter that made her bitter butter batter better.

WIN MONEY OR EAT BUGS!

Directions: Find the twelve bugs Miss Laney ate on the TV show *Win Money or Eat Bugs!* in the jumble of letters below.

```
Z A T P I L T V X A N Y R O M
A N R D O L T C M O U U T M O
P G R A S S H O P P E R P I S
L C Z P P R N C D H T T B L Q
G K P A I I U K Y S E E S K U
R E Y G D T H R R D R R L Y I
A R L Q E K C O S E F F U W T
W S B O R A L A D Y B U G A O
O E M A G T R C I N N N B Y S
R D N F L A G H B L G A N T T
M M O R N T D G E V E Q S V F
C U C E N T I P E D E O T H L
T A B U G E L T T I V E L I Y
B O N M J D F K L U D B O Y O
L W A C R I C K E T I X Y I G
```

cricket   spider   slug
mosquito   fly   beetle   worm
cockroach   grasshopper   ant
ladybug   centipede

FUN AT RECESS

Directions: Circle the things Mrs. Lizzy DIDN'T teach A.J. and the gang during recess enrichment. (Hint: The answers can be found in *My Weird School Daze #9: Mrs. Lizzy Is Dizzy!*)

1. How to make balloon animals
2. How to milk Pootie the goat
3. How to make a banjo out of toothpicks
4. How to yodel
5. How to play the ukulele
6. How to make armpit farts
7. Worm composting
8. How to ride a unicycle

MISS MARY'S RIDDLEGRAM

Directions: Chip, chip, cheerio! Solve the riddlegram below to find out what Miss Mary and her boyfriend, Zack, like to do for fun back home in England.

Fill in the answers to the clues, one letter in each blank. Then transfer the letters to the boxes that have the same numbers. When all the boxes are filled in correctly, you will have the answer.

1	2	3		4	5	6	7	8	9	10	11	12	13

A. This covers your whole body

$\overline{}_{4}\ \overline{}_{8}\ \overline{}_{11}\ \overline{}_{5}$

B. Something gross that comes out of your nose

$\overline{}_{1}\ \overline{}_{2}\ \overline{}_{6}\ \overline{}_{3}\ \overline{}_{9}\ \overline{}_{7}$

C. Something short stories are not

$\overline{}_{10}\ \overline{}_{2}\ \overline{}_{12}\ \overline{}_{13}$

WHAT DO YOU LIKE ON YOUR PIZZA?

Directions: Mr. Tony and the kids of Ella Mentry School are going to create the world's largest pizza to get into *The Guinness Book of World Records*! What toppings should they put on it? Find twelve possibilities in the jumble of letters below.

```
Z S V E Y P O P O T B B A J Y
A N P D O L P I N E A P P L E
W Z E L E S V X I O T T P A R
L A P R C B A L O N E Y B L Z
G I P A T I N F N S E E R O T
R E E G Q T C A S A L A M I Z
A V R E S K H A S M F F T X E
P T O M A T O S A U C E C R N
L P N A U T V A I S H N H Y S
A I I F S A I E N H E A E P T
M L U N A S E G H R V Q E V X
C U F J G P S I R O S U S H O
T A H E E S H E Y O E R E I L
B O N M J D F H A M D B S Y T
P E P P E R S U T S M P T I M
```

pepperoni salami baloney
sausage cheese mushrooms
tomato sauce anchovies
pineapple ham onions
peppers

51

THE SECRET MATH LESSON

Directions: Mr. Granite is always trying to do the lesson on page twenty-three of the math book, but he keeps getting interrupted. Would you like to see the lesson that's on page twenty-three?

Well, we're not going to show it to you. So nah-nah-nah boo-boo on you! But here are some weird math word problems. . . . (Okay, maybe they're jokes!)

1. If you multiply a chicken times a walrus and subtract three chimpanzees, what do you get?
2. If A.J. eats 3 Twinkies, 2 Ring Dings, 12 ice cream pops, 87 candy bars, and a piece of apple pie, what does he end up with?
3. How many Ella Mentry School teachers does it take to screw in a lightbulb?
4. A.J. is more annoying than Ryan, and Ryan is more annoying than Michael and Alexia. Michael and Andrea are equally annoying, but Emily is more annoying than Andrea. Which student is the most annoying?
5. Spiders have 8 legs. There are 4 quarters in a dollar. Little Miss Muffet sat on 1 tuffet. So how many helicopters does it take to make 1 toothbrush?

MR. SLUG'S SECRET MESSAGE

Directions: Mr. Slug is the world's unhealthiest robot! He eats junk food, never exercises, and doesn't get enough sleep. Use this secret code to swap in letters below to read Mr. Slug's message.

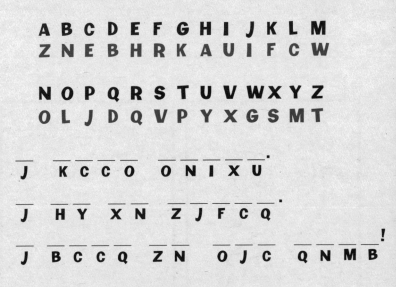

A	B	C	D	E	F	G	H	I	J	K	L	M
Z	N	E	B	H	R	K	A	U	I	F	C	W

N	O	P	Q	R	S	T	U	V	W	X	Y	Z
O	L	J	D	Q	V	P	Y	X	G	S	M	T

_ _ _ _ _ _ _ _ _ _ .
J   K C C O   O N I X U

_ _ _ _ _ _ _ _ _ _ .
J   H Y   X N   Z J F C Q

_ _ _ _ _ _ _ _ _ _ _ _ !
J   B C C Q   Z N   O J C   Q N M B

cough! cough!

DRAW AND COLOR
LIKE CRAZY!

All the color has gone out of Andrea's face! It's a catastrophe!* You don't know what to say! You don't know what to do! You've got to think fast! Quick, grab some pencils or crayons! Draw Andrea in the empty box below. Then color in the cover on the right.

*That's when a cat eats an apostrophe.

SPOT THE DIFFERENCES

Directions: Do you have sharp eyes? Wow, I guess that means you're always stabbing things with your face! Well, if your eyes are so sharp, see if you can spot the differences in these two covers. (Hint: There are six.)

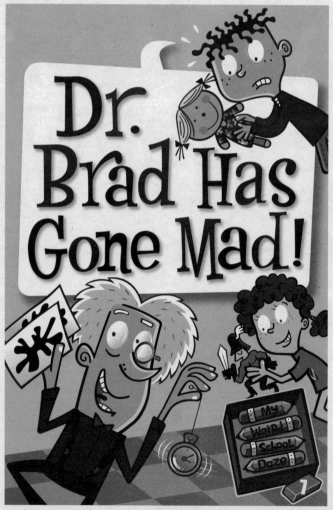

WACKY WORD STORY TIME

Directions: Before you read this story, fill in each blank with a word that fits the description next to it. After you've filled in all the blanks, go back and read the story out loud. Is it funny? Or just really weird?

Did I ever tell you about the big peanut butter and jelly sandwich robbery at school? Oh, you should have been there! Here's what happened. Me and the gang were in the vomitorium eating lunch. Ryan had a _____ (*noun*). Michael had a _____ (*noun*). Neil had two _____ (*plural noun*). I went to open my _____ (*noun*) box. And guess what was inside?

I'm not going to tell you. Okay, okay, I'll tell you.

Nothing! My _____ (*same as previous word*) box was empty!

What?! My mom *never* forgets to pack my peanut butter and jelly sandwich! I turned my _____ (*same as previous word*) box upside down just to make sure the sandwich wasn't stuck to the bottom.

"Okay, which one of you _____ (*plural noun*) stole my _____ (*noun*)?" I asked.

"Not me," they all said.

That's when the weirdest thing in the history of the _____ (*noun*) happened. Our security guard, Officer Spence, came _____ (*verb*)-ing over. He gets to carry cool stuff on his belt—a_____ (*noun*), a _____ (*noun*), a _____ (*noun*), and one of those big _____ (*plural noun*) they use to beat up bad guys.

"Did I hear something about a stolen _____ (*noun*)?" Officer Spence said.

He grabbed his _____ (*noun*) and started shouting into it. "We have a Code Red at Ella Mentry School! A _____ (*noun*) robbery! Somebody stole a _____ (*noun*). This is an emergency!"

"But, Officer Spence, really, I don't need—"

I never had the chance to finish my _____ (*noun*), because that's when _____ (*number*) big _____ (*plural noun*) came _____ (*verb*)-ing into the vomitorium. They were carrying _____ (*plural noun*)! They surrounded our table. It was scary, but cool too.

"Nobody move!" Officer Spence shouted. He took a _____ (*noun*) out of his pocket and wrapped it around our _____ (*plural noun*). "Don't touch anything!" he said. "This is a crime scene. Nobody leave this _____ (*noun*)."

Everybody in the vomitorium was _____ (*verb*)-ing and freaking out. That's when Mr. Klutz came _____ (*verb*)-ing in. He's our principal, and he has no _____ (*noun*) at all. I mean *none*. His _____ (*noun*) is so shiny, you can see yourself in it. Mr. Klutz was eating a _____ (*noun*).

"Is there a problem here?" he asked.

Suddenly Officer Spence wheeled around and pointed his _____ (*noun*) at Mr. Klutz, just like policemen do to bad guys on TV.

"Freeze, dirtbag!" he yelled. Mr. Klutz put his _____ (*plural noun*) in the air.

"Step away from the _____ (*noun*), Klutz, and nobody gets hurt!" Officer Spence said. "You're under arrest!"

It was cool. Later, Officer Spence arrested all the teachers and threw them in jail. I could tell you more, but you should just read *Officer Spence Makes No Sense!* instead. So nah-nah-nah boo-boo on you!

MY WEIRD SCHOOL DAZE TRIVIA

There's no way in a million hundred years you'll get all these answers right. So nah-nah-nah boo-boo on you! (Hint: All the answers to the questions below come from the My Weird School Daze series.)

Q: WHO WAS THE SPECIAL GUEST SPEAKER AT ELLA MENTRY SCHOOL'S SECOND-GRADE GRADUATION?

A: President Bill Clinton

Q: WHAT DOES A.J. THINK MISS DAISY AND MR. MACKY'S BABY SHOULD BE NAMED?

A: Hydrant

Q: WHAT IS MR. SUNNY'S REAL NAME?

A: Evan

Q: WHAT DID ANDREA BRING TO THE BEACH FOR SUMMER READING?

A: *The Complete Works of Shakespeare*

Q: WHAT STORE DOES A.J. THINK IS THE BORINGEST IN THE HISTORY OF THE WORLD?

A: Staples

Q: MR. GRANITE STARTS A NEW PROGRAM CALLED PAL. WHAT DOES PAL STAND FOR?

A: Pedal and Learn

Q: WHAT IS THE NAME OF A.J.'S PEE WEE FOOTBALL TEAM?

A: The Moose

Q: WHAT HAPPENED TO COACH HYATT'S HAMSTER, CHIP?

A: He got run over by a bulldozer.

Q: WHAT ARE THE NAMES OF MRS. JAFEE'S PEANUT BUTTER–SNIFFING DOGS?

A: Skippy and Jif

Q: WHAT IS THE NAME OF THE YOGA TEACHER MRS. JAFEE HIRES?

A: Swami Havabanana

Q: WHAT IS THE NAME OF MRS. JAFEE'S NEW KITTEN?

A: Mister Fur Columbus

Q: IN WHAT ROOM DOES DR. BRAD TEST A.J.?

A: Room 104

Q: WHERE IS MISS LANEY'S OFFICE?

A: The girls' bathroom

Q: WHAT IS THE NAME OF MISS LANEY'S PUPPET?

A: Ollie the Octopus

Q: WHO IS THE HOST OF THE GAME SHOW *WIN MONEY OR EAT BUGS!*?

A: Dickie Blinkbarker

Q: WHAT IS THE NAME OF MISS MARY'S PET BAT?

A: Roger

Q: WHAT IS THE NAME OF THE HIT SONG MISS MARY'S BOYFRIEND, ZACK, WROTE?

A: "I Love Dirt"

Q: WHY DOES MR. KLUTZ HAVE SOLAR PANELS ON HIS HAT?

A: To power his pencil sharpener

Q: HOW DOES MR. TONY COOK THE PIZZA CRUST ON THE PLAYGROUND?

A: With a flamethrower

Q: WHAT DID MRS. LIZZY STUDY IN COLLEGE?

A: Balloon animal construction

Q: WHAT IS THE NAME OF MS. LEAKEY'S RESTAURANT?

A: McLeakey's

Q: WHAT WAS MS. LEAKEY'S PUNCHING BAG FILLED WITH?

A: Candy

PART 3

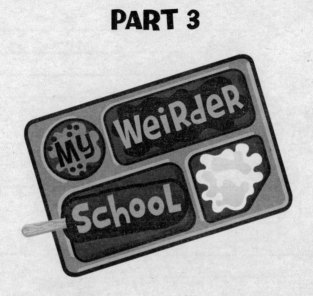

THIS PLACE IS A ZOO!

Directions: A.J. and Andrea are on a class trip to the zoo. Help them find their way to Penguin Paradise to visit A.J.'s favorite animal!

ZOO ZONES

Directions: Name the animal habitats at the zoo by matching the words below. To get you started, we did the first one for you!

1. LION __LANE__ _____

2. TURTLE _____

3. ALLIGATOR _____

4. LIZARD _____

5. RHINO _____

6. BAT _____

7. ZEBRA _____

8. SNAKE _____

9. HEDGEHOG _____

10. PENGUIN ——————

Highway   Street   Lane   Zone   Avenue
Boulevard   Road   Paradise   Town

WHO'S WHO AT
ELLA MENTRY SCHOOL?

Directions: See how well you know the kids by matching the names below with their description.

I. **NEVER TIES HIS SHOES** _____

2. **WILL EAT ANYTHING, EVEN STUFF THAT ISN'T FOOD** _____

3. **THE NUDE KID** _____

4. **CRYBABY** _____

5. **LITTLE MISS PERFECT** _____

6. **SKATEBOARDING TOMBOY** _____

7. **LIVES AROUND THE CORNER FROM A.J.**

_____

8. **IS ALWAYS PICKING HIS NOSE** _____

9. **A.J.'S SISTER** _____

IO. **HATES SCHOOL** _____

**Wyatt Andrea Neil Michael Alexia
Billy A.J. Ryan Amy Emily**

MR. FIX-IT WORD SCRAMBLE

Directions: Mr. Harrison is embarrassin', but he can fix anything! Unscramble the letters below to find things he fixes at Ella Mentry School.

1. FECOFE CHEMINA _____

2. PROMCUTE _____

3. RALES RENTRIP _____

4. TERMCOIN _____

5. CLENIP PRESHNEAR _____

6. COINHORMEP _____

7. PYOC HENICAM _____

8. MARST DRABO _____

FAKE NEWS

Directions: The school newspaper, *The Ella Mentry Sentry*, needs to grab readers' eyeballs (Ouch! That's gotta hurt!), so the kids start writing crazy stories! Match the fake headlines below to their real stories.

1. MS. COCO IS A CAR THIEF!! _____

2. MR. KLUTZ HAS TWO WIVES!! _____

3. MRS. YONKERS SETS FIRES FOR FUN!!
_____

4. MR. MACKY SPOTTED KISSING MARRIED WOMAN!! _____

5. OFFICER SPENCE WAS IN JAIL FOR FIVE YEARS!! _____

A. This teacher borrowed a car to get to school when hers broke down.
B. This teacher has backyard barbecues every weekend.
C. These teachers, who are married to each other, kissed near the water fountain.
D. This person was married, divorced, and then remarried.
E. Before he worked at Ella Mentry School, this person was a prison guard.

71

ELEVEN TIMES TABLE

A.J.'s friend Billy told him that if you multiply 11 x 11, you get sucked into a parallel universe and travel through time until your head explodes. Try it and see what happens!

11 x 1 = _____   11 x 7 = _____

11 x 2 = _____   11 x 8 = _____

11 x 3 = _____   11 x 9 = _____

11 x 4 = _____   11 x 10 = _____

11 x 5 = _____   11 x 11 = _____

11 x 6 = _____

YEE-HA!

Directions: It's gold fever at Ella Mentry School when Mr. Burke discovers gilver (a combination of gold and silver) under the playground. Dig up twelve Wild West words in the jumble of letters below.

```
M S V E Y P O P H T B B A J Y
A N R D O V A R M I N T D M N
W I C L E S V X N O T A F N R
L M A L P S U D S M O R B U Z
G P P T P C F Y S P C N U G T
R D A G N A B I T D R A K G Z
A L R G K L A S E L F T V E E
P B D G I L V E R B I I W T N
R M N G T Y A I O M N O O Y S
A D E E N W W C B L G N X P T
S O R R V A M O O S E Y S V X
C U F J A G G O R Y R U T H O
A A H E R S H T J R E C K O N
L O N M J D F K S U D B O Y T
O M L N V P W Z V I T T L E S
```

vamoose   pardner   tarnation   dagnabit
gilver   coot   rascal   scallywag   varmint
nugget   reckon   vittles

SAVE MISS KRAFT'S LIFE!

Directions: If A.J.'s class can't list all fifty states in ABC order, a five-hundred-pound weight is going to drop on Miss Kraft's head! Can they do it? Can YOU do it? You have five minutes. Go!

South Carolina	Maine	Missouri
Massachusetts	New Hampshire	Illinois
Mississippi	North Dakota	North Carolina
West Virginia	Indiana	Wyoming
Ohio	Colorado	Montana
Kentucky	Delaware	New York
Georgia	Tennessee	Nevada
Michigan	Alabama	Kansas
Rhode Island	Oregon	Arizona
Pennsylvania	Maryland	Hawaii
Iowa	Louisiana	Utah
Minnesota	Washington	South Dakota
Connecticut	Nebraska	Texas
Vermont	Oklahoma	Florida
Arkansas	Alaska	New Mexico
Wisconsin	Virginia	California
Idaho	New Jersey	

The fifty states in alphabetical order:

1. _____
2. _____
3. _____
4. _____
5. _____
6. _____
7. _____
8. _____
9. _____
10. _____
11. _____
12. _____
13. _____
14. _____
15. _____
16. _____
17. _____
18. _____
19. _____
20. _____
21. _____
22. _____
23. _____
24. _____
25. _____

26. _____
27. _____
28. _____
29. _____
30. _____
31. _____
32. _____
33. _____
34. _____
35. _____
36. _____
37. _____
38. _____
39. _____
40. _____
41. _____
42. _____
43. _____
44. _____
45. _____
46. _____
47. _____
48. _____
49. _____
50. _____

WHAT IS A.J.'S FAVORITE SUBJECT?

Directions: The scrambled words below are all school subjects at Ella Mentry School. Unscramble the five words. Reading top to bottom, A.J.'s favorite period of the day will be spelled out by the circled letters.

GEDNIRA ⬤ __ __ __ __ __ __

ICESNCE __ __ __ __ __ __ ⬤

HAMTATECISM __ __ __ __ __ __ __ __ __ ⬤ __

ZIZF DE __ __ __ __ ⬤ __

OILCAS SUITEDS ⬤ __ __ __ __ __

__ __ __ __ __ ⬤ __

Answer: __ __ __ __ __ __

AJ'S CAMPAIGN PROMISES

A.J. is running for third-grade class president. Which of the campaign promises below did he make? Circle *Y* or *N*. (Hint: All the answers can be found in *My Weirder School #6: Mayor Hubble Is in Trouble!*)

1. Abolish homework. **Y N**
2. Kids will wear school uniforms. **Y N**
3. Every day will be a snow day. **Y N**
4. There will be fewer fire drills. **Y N**
5. Abolish anything higher than the five times table. **Y N**
6. Teachers will be replaced by comic book superheroes. **Y N**
7. Water fountains will be filled with lemonade. **Y N**
8. A video game system will be built into every desk. **Y N**

TEACHERS ARE HILARIOUS!

It's time for your favorite TV show, *The Real Teachers of Ella Mentry School.* The teachers sing, dance, mud wrestle, and tell jokes to win a vacation to anywhere in the world, plus a year's supply of Porky's pork sausages! Here are a few quick jokes from the finalists. . . .

MR. GRANITE

WHAT DID THE ALIEN SAY TO THE GAS PUMP?
Take your finger out of your nose while I speak to you.

WHY DON'T ALIENS EAT CLOWNS?
They taste funny.

WHY DID THE RESTAURANT ON THE MOON GO OUT OF BUSINESS?
It had no atmosphere.

MR. MACKY

THE OTHER DAY A BOOK FELL ON MY HEAD.
Well, I only have my shelf to blame.

WHAT HAS A SPINE BUT NO BONES?
A book!

MISS SMALL

WHY DO BABIES LIKE BASKETBALLS?
Because they're so good at dribbling

WHICH ANIMAL IS GOOD AT HITTING A BASEBALL?
A bat

WHY IS CINDERELLA A LOUSY SOCCER PLAYER?
Because she always runs away from the ball

MS. LEAKY

AN APPLE A DAY KEEPS THE DOCTOR AWAY.
Well, only if you have good aim.

WHY DID THE TOMATO GO OUT WITH A PRUNE?
Because he couldn't find a date

WHY DID THE LETTUCE BLUSH?
Because it saw the salad dressing

DR. NICHOLAS'S RIDICULOUS CROSSWORD PUZZLE

Directions: Fill in the answers below with historical (and sometimes ridiculous) things the kids learn from Dr. Nicholas.

Across

3. She sewed the first American flag.
5. How we choose between candidates
6. What Dr. Nicholas teaches
7. The name of Dr. Nicholas's time machine

Down

1. He opened the first toilet bowl store.
2. Place where teachers teach and kids learn
4. Inventor of the lightbulb

MY WEIRD DOGS

Directions: Miss Klute, the school therapy dog, is a hoot! She's also a labradoodle—a combination of Labrador retriever and poodle. Match the combinations below to their actual dog breed name.

1. **CHIHUAHUA + DACHSHUND =** _____

2. **SCHNAUZER + YORKIE =** _____

3. **PAPILLON + POODLE =** _____

4. **DACHSHUND + POODLE =** _____

5. **COLLIE + POODLE =** _____

6. **CHIHUAHUA + PUG =** _____

7. **SCHNAUZER + POODLE =** _____

8. **BULLDOG + WHIPPET =** _____

schnoodle   chiweenie   doxiepoo   snorkie
chug   cadoodle   papi-poo   bullwhip

HOW TALENTED ARE YOU?

Directions: Hidden in the jumble of letters below, find twelve things that the kids and teachers performed at the Ella Mentry School talent show.

```
M S V E Y P O P H T B B A J Y
J N R D O N O S E F L U T E N
U Y O D E L I N G O X E P I R
G C M X L V D U L T T A B L Z
G K A R M P I T F A R T S J T
L E G G Q T H A R P R I O O Z
I R I E G K C A S D F N T K E
N S C O N A T R A A I G L E N
G E T A G T R A I N N B B S H
B U R P I N G E N C G U D P T
M O I N D S D G H I E G S S X
C U C J A P B A B N R S T K O
T A K R A P P I N G A R T I L
B O S M J D F K S U D B O T T
L I P S Y N C H I N G S K S P
```

magic tricks   nose flute   yodeling
armpit farts   juggling   jokes   tap dancing
eating bugs   skits   lip synching   rapping
burping

MANAGE YOUR MONEY

Directions: Help A.J. move just THREE coins to flip this triangle upside down.

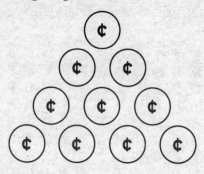

Directions: These nine coins form a triangle. Help A.J. move just TWO coins to form a square.

THE SECRET CARNIVAL CODE

Directions: It's time for the annual Ella Mentry School carnival! Use this secret code to swap in letters below and find out some of this year's wackiest carnival games.

A	B	C	D	E	F	G	H	I	J	K	L	M
Z	N	E	B	H	R	K	A	U	I	F	C	W

N	O	P	Q	R	S	T	U	V	W	X	Y	Z
O	L	J	D	Q	V	P	Y	X	G	S	M	T

_ _ _ _ _ _   _ _ _ _   _ _ _ _
Z N J O C Z   X C H Z   Z N X X

_ _ _ _ _ _ _   _ _ _ _ _
W N H Z J B W   D N N Z E

_ _ _   _ _ _   _ _ _ _ _
D J W   L H F   X Y H X E

_ _ _   _ _ _   _ _ _ _ _
L N M   T J C   D J B W N

_ _ _ _   _ _ _ _ _
G J X X   H Z N H Q

DRAW AND COLOR
LIKE CRAZY!

Oh no! This must be contagious! All the color
has gone out of Alexia's face! She's pale as a
ghost! Quick, grab some pencils or crayons!
Draw Alexia in the empty box below, then color
in the cover on the right. Save these kids from
a dismal black-and-white world before it's too
late!*

*Why are you wasting your time looking down here?
Start coloring!

SPOT THE DIFFERENCES

Directions: These two covers are identical. Well, *almost*. There are six differences. Can you spot them?

My WEiRDeR School 9

Ms. Sue Has No Clue!

Dan Gutman

Pictures by
Jim Paillot

WACKY WORD STORY TIME

Directions: Before you read this story, fill in each blank with a word that fits the description next to it. After you've filled in all the blanks, go back and read the story out loud. Is it funny? Or just really weird?

My name is A.J. and I hate getting hit in the head with a _____ (*noun*).

Did you and your friends ever have a _____ (*noun*) fight? That is the coolest sport in the history of the _____ (*noun*). Especially when you do it while you're standing on a _____ (*noun*).

One time, we were having a battle on the _____ (*noun*) next to our _____ (*noun*). My friend Alexia and I climbed on our _____ (*plural noun*) at opposite ends of the _____ (*noun*). Ryan and Michael put a line of orange _____ (*plural thing*) on the _____ (*noun*) so Alexia and I wouldn't crash into each other.

I put my _____ (*noun*) on my head. Alexia put her _____ (*noun*) on her head.

"Hand me my _____ (*noun*)," I told Neil.

Neil handed me a big red _____ (*noun*). I saw Emily hand Alexia a blue _____ (*noun*) at the other end of the field.

"Are you ready?" shouted Neil.

"Ready!" Alexia and I shouted.

"On your mark . . . ," yelled Neil. "Get set! Start
_____ (*verb*)-ing!"

Alexia and I started _____ (*verb*)-ing toward
each other. It's not easy to _____ (*verb*) a
_____ (*noun*) on the_____ (*noun*) while
you're holding a _____ (*noun*) in one hand.

We were getting closer to each other.

I held up my _____ (*noun*), ready to let it fly.

Alexia and I were _____ (*number*) feet away
from each other.

It's really hard to hit somebody with a _____
(*noun*) from a moving _____ (*noun*). You
have to throw it at the exact perfect moment.

Alexia and I were _____ (*number*) feet away
from each other. It was time.

"_____ (*exclamation*)!" I hollered.

Just as I was about to let go of my _____
(*noun*), Alexia heaved her _____ (*noun*) at
me. It exploded all over my _____ (*noun*).

"_____ (*exclamation*)!" Alexia hollered as she
rode by. "In your _____ (*noun*), A.J.!"

"Alexia is the _____ (*noun*)!" shouted Neil.

It was a blast! I got nailed _____ (*number*) times, but I hit Alexia a few times too. Everybody was falling all over each other laughing. We kept _____ (*verb*)-ing until we ran out of _____ (*plural noun*).

That's when the most amazing thing in the history of the _____ (*noun*) happened. I noticed that somebody was hiding behind a _____ (*noun*) nearby.

It was Mr. Klutz, our school principal!

He has no _____ (*noun*) at all. I mean *none*. He must save a lot of money on shampoo and _____ (*noun*). I wonder if he uses a _____ (*noun*) to dry his _____ (*noun*).

"Uh-oh!" I said. "It's Mr. Klutz!"

Mr. Klutz came over to us.

"We're sorry, Mr. Klutz," I said. "We won't do it again."

"Please don't tell our parents we were _____ (*verb*)-ing with _____ (*plural noun*)," begged Neil.

"Don't be silly!" said Mr. Klutz, with a big _____ (*noun*) on his face. "I enjoyed watching you. When I was a kid, my friends and I used to throw _____ (*plural noun*) at each other all the time."

Mr. Klutz is weird.

MY WEIRDER SCHOOL TRIVIA

Okay, you've been pretty lucky so far. But there's no way in a million hundred years you'll get all these answers right. (Hint: All the answers to the questions below come from the My Weirder School series.)

Q: WHAT IS ALEXIA'S LAST NAME?

A: Juarez

Q: WHAT IS THE NAME OF THE ELEPHANT THAT PAINTS AT THE ZOO?

A: Binky

Q: WHAT DID MR. HARRISON INVENT THAT WAS A DUMB IDEA?

A: A solar-powered umbrella

Q: WHAT PROFESSIONAL SKATEBOARDER VISITED ELLA MENTRY SCHOOL ON CAREER DAY?

A: Tony Eagle

Q: WITH THE NEW SCHOOL BUDGET CUTS, WHAT WILL BE USED FOR TOILET PAPER?

A: Post-it notes

Q: WHAT KIND OF RACE DOES MR. BURKE HAVE WITH MR. KLUTZ?

A: A lawn mower race

Q: WHAT ARE THE TWO TEAMS MS. BEARD DIVIDES THE SCHOOL INTO?

A: The Mooseketeers and the Hot Dog Heads

Q: WHAT DOES MR. KLUTZ'S UNDERPANTS LOOK LIKE?

A: Pink boxer shorts with red hearts

Q: WHAT IS THE NAME OF MR. GRANITE'S STUNT TEACHER?

A: Brownie the Clownie

Q: WHAT SECRET DID ANDREA WRITE IN HER PRIVATE DIARY?

A: I like A.J.

Q: WHERE DID MISS KRAFT GO TO COLLEGE?
A: Clown College

Q: WHAT IS THE NAME OF MISS KRAFT'S SOCK PUPPET?
A: Mr. Bongo

Q: HOW OLD IS DR. NICHOLAS?
A: 92

Q: WHO DID A.J. SAY INVENTED THE LIGHTBULB ON HIS HISTORY TEST?
A: Bob Lightbulb

Q: WHAT IS THE NAME OF THE STUDY GROUP THE KIDS FORM TO PASS THEIR HISTORY TEST?
A: Study Buddies

Q: WHAT DOES MR. JACK SAY THE KIDS CAN CALL HIM?
A: Mr. Jack

Q: WHAT DOES MR. JACK MAKE THE KIDS WEAR TO PROTECT THEMSELVES?
A: Helmets, pads, and bubble wrap

Q: WHAT DID MISS KLUTE EAT IN THE TEACHERS' LOUNGE THAT MADE HER SICK?
A: Chocolate cupcakes

Q: WHAT DOES A.J. NAME THE GOLDFISH HE WON AT THE SCHOOL CARNIVAL?

A: Fishy T. Fish

Q: WHO WON THE SCHOOL CARNIVAL BEAUTY PAGEANT?

A: Mr. Tony

Q: WHAT WAS MRS. LANE RIDING WHEN THE KIDS FIRST MET HER?

A: A unicycle

Q: WHO IS THE SPECIAL GUEST STAR AT *ELLA MENTRY SCHOOL'S GOT TALENT*?

A: The rapper Cray-Z

PART 4

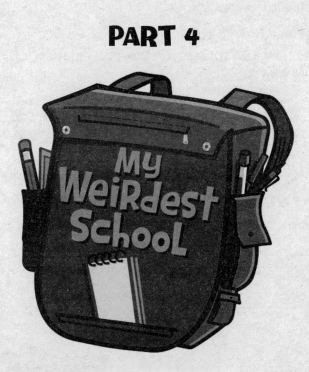

A.J. AND ANDREA SITTING IN A TREE

Directions: *"Ooo!"* said Ryan, "A.J. and Andrea must be in *love*!"

"When are you gonna get married?" asked Michael. Use this secret code to swap in letters and find out what A.J. *really* thinks.

A	B	C	D	E	F	G	H	I	J	K	L	M
Z	N	E	B	H	R	K	A	U	I	F	C	W

N	O	P	Q	R	S	T	U	V	W	X	Y	Z
O	L	J	D	Q	V	P	Y	X	G	S	M	T

—— ——
J K   Z E N X C   W I U X

,

—— —— ——
M C F C B Z   Y U   D C X Z

——'
K F J C B Q X

——
J M N I O Q

——!
E H Z C   Z E C Y

MORE WHO'S WHO?

Directions: Match the names with what they do at Ella Mentry School.

1. **NEW THIRD-GRADE TEACHER** _____

2. **DIGITAL MEDIA ARTS TEACHER** _____

3. **BRAIN GAMES COACH** _____

4. **FIREFIGHTER** _____

5. **SUBSTITUTE TEACHER** _____

6. **NEW PRINCIPAL** _____

7. **SCHOOL PHOTOGRAPHER** _____

8. **ALEXIA'S GRANDMOTHER/INVENTOR**

_____

9. **MISS UNIVERSE** _____

**Mrs. Master   Miss Brown   Mr. Cooper
Mr. Nick   Miss Tracy   Ms. Cuddy
Miss Daisy   Ms. Joni   Mrs. Meyer**

PIZZA MATH

Directions: Mr. Cooper is super! One of his superpowers is that he can use pizza to teach math. Can you solve his pizza problems below?

1. Each pizza topping costs 50 cents extra. How much would a pizza that normally costs $10 cost if you added pepperoni, mushrooms, sausage, anchovies, and bacon?

2. A pizza delivery boy has 5 pizzas to deliver to 5 houses, and it takes him 12 minutes to get to each house. How long will it take him to deliver all the pizzas?

3. A pizza is cut into 8 slices. You and your sister each eat a slice. Your dad eats 2 slices, and your mom has a salad. How much pizza will you have left over?

4. Another pizza is cut into 8 slices. You flip it in the air and it sticks to the ceiling. One slice falls off and then another. How much of the pizza is still stuck to the ceiling?

WORLD WAR WEIRD!

Directions: Ella Mentry School and Dirk School are having a TV news war! Match the school to the weird things they do to get big ratings. (Hint: All the answers can be found in *My Weirdest School #2: Ms. Cuddy Is Nutty!*)

ELLA
MENTRY OR DIRK

I. SINGS SONGS FROM *ANNIE* _____ _____

2. CLOG DANCES ON TOP OF
NEWS DESK _____ _____

3. RE-CREATES MICHAEL
JACKSON'S "THRILLER" VIDEO _____ _____

4. PUTS PARENTS ON TV _____ _____

5. PLAYS *WIN MONEY OR EAT
BUGS!* REALITY SHOW _____ _____

6. STAGES A ZOMBIE-AND-
VAMPIRE ATTACK _____ _____

7. PLAYS *KILLER KARAOKE*
REALITY SHOW _____ _____

BRAIN GAMES CAR MAZE

Directions: It's time for the Brain Games!
Navigate the Ella Mentry School car, the Death
Machine, through the maze to the Bridge of Love.

ONLY YOU CAN PREVENT FOREST FIRES!

Directions: Well, actually, anybody can. That's what Woodsy the Bear says, and he ought to know. Answer the questions below using only the letters in:

WOODSY THE BEAR

1. LIQUID SOAP YOU USE IN THE SHOWER

_____

2. THESE ARE ABOVE YOUR EYES ON YOUR FACE _____

3. TO BRAG _____

4. THE PLANET WE LIVE ON _____

5. A TYPE OF SHELLFISH _____

6. KIND OF HAT THEY WEAR IN FRANCE

_____

7. SOMETHING YOU USE IN SEWING

_____

MRS. MEYER'S FIRE RULES

Directions: Mrs. Meyer is on fire!
Use this secret code to swap in letters below and learn her fire rules.

A	B	C	D	E	F	G	H	I	J	K	L	M
Z	N	E	B	H	R	K	A	U	I	F	C	W

N	O	P	Q	R	S	T	U	V	W	X	Y	Z
O	L	J	D	Q	V	P	Y	X	G	S	M	T

1. What should you do if your clothes catch on fire?

X Z N T '   Q F N T '   H B Q   F N O O

2. What should you do if your bedroom is on fire?

K H O O   H B Q   L F H M O

3. What should you do if there's a fire in your house?

'

Q N B Z   E J Q C .

WN   N I Z X J Q C .

104

GERM WARFARE

Directions: The school nurse, Mrs. Cooney, is loony! She thinks germs are everywhere! Unscramble the letters below to find the most common places we find them.

1. ODORBONKS _____

2. SEABIB _____

3. OTITLE ASTES _____

4. HOTELSNEEP _____

5. ABBY SOYT _____

6. KANESSER _____

7. CHINKET UNCROTE _____

8. NASHD _____

WHAT'S WRONG WITH MR. COOPER?

Directions: Yikes! Mr. Cooper has a horrible disease called onychocryptosis, so the class will need a substitute teacher. Solve the riddlegram below to find out a simpler name for what's wrong with Mr. Cooper. Fill in the answers to the clues, one letter in each blank. Then transfer the letters to the boxes that have the same numbers. When all the boxes are filled in correctly, you'll have the answer.

1	2	3	4	5	6	7		8	9	10	11	12	13	14

A. Adjective that means "doesn't know anything" __ __ __ __ __ __ __ __
   1   3   2   5   4   12   11   8

B. Something you just got is __ __ __
   7   10   6

C. Liquid used to fry food __ __ __
   9   13   14

ONYCHOCRYPTOSIS

NO COFFEE!

Directions: Oh no! The coffee machine in the teachers' lounge is on the fritz, and all the grown-ups are freaking out! Find fourteen coffee-themed words in the jumble of letters below.

```
T S V E Y P O P H T B B A J Y
A N R D O L C A M O U U C M N
S I C C R E A M E R T T U I R
U C M G H K P A I S T T P L Z
G K F R A P P U C C I N O K T
A E G O Q T U A R I R R F Y Z
R R L U D E C A F E F F J W B
P S B N N H C R A R I P O A E
L E M D G T I A I O N N E Y A
A D N S L A N E N L G A D P N
M B J D W M O C H A E J S V S
C R F J A P H A D T W A Z H O
T E S P R E S S O T A V T I L
D W N M C O F F E E M A K E R
O J U S E O R P Z N Y T C L O
```

Must have Coffee...

brew   java   sugar   coffee maker
cappuccino   cup of joe   decaf
creamer   Frappuccino   mocha
grounds   beans   latte   espresso

107

LOVEY-DOVEY SCRAMBLE

Directions: Miss Daisy and Mr. Macky are in love, love, LOVE! Unscramble the letters below to find their pet names for each other.

1. **GLEAN FINFUM** _____ _____

2. **GRUSALUMP** _____

3. **GLINRAD** _____

4. **EWESTEARTH** _____

5. **NOHEY UNB** _____ _____

6. **EWETIES EPI** _____ _____

7. **URGAS SILP** _____ _____

WHAT DID RYAN WEAR ON PICTURE DAY?

Directions: There's only one way to find out. Draw a picture in the grid below by shading in the squares as indicated. For example, in Row 1, shade in the squares in Columns H, I, J, and K. When you're done, the picture you made will reveal the answer.

	A	B	C	D	E	F	G	H	I	J	K	L	M	N	O
1															
2															
3															
4															
5															
6															
7															
8															
9															

Row 1: **HIJK**

Row 2: **ABCDHKL**

Row 3: **ADLM**

Row 4: **DEMN**

Row 5: **EFNO**

Row 6: **FGHIJKLMNO**

Row 7: **GHIJLMNO**

Row 8: **GHIJLMNO**

Row 9: **GHIJLMNO**

109

A.J.'S TOILET JOKES!

Ugh, disgusting! Gross! That's what grown-ups say about toilet humor. Well, here are some toilet jokes that will gross out your parents. So nah-nah-nah *poo-poo* on them.

WHY DID THE SUPERHERO FLUSH THE TOILET?

Because it was his doody

IF YOU'RE AMERICAN IN THE LIVING ROOM, WHAT ARE YOU IN THE BATHROOM?

Euro-peein'

WHY DID THE TOILET PAPER ROLL DOWN THE HILL?

To get to the bottom

WHY COULDN'T THE TOILET PAPER CROSS THE ROAD?

It got stuck in a crack.

WHY DID THE ELEPHANT BRING TOILET PAPER TO A PARTY?

Because he's a party pooper

WHY CAN'T YOU HEAR A PTERODACTYL WHEN IT'S IN THE BATHROOM?

Because the p is silent

WHAT WOULD YOU FIND IN SUPERMAN'S BATHROOM?

A Super Bowl

WHAT DO YOU CALL A FAIRY USING THE TOILET?

Stinker Bell

WHAT DID ONE TOILET SAY TO THE OTHER TOILET?

You look flushed.

WHY DID TIGGER STICK HIS HEAD IN THE TOILET?

He was looking for Pooh.

WHAT ARE TWO REASONS NEVER TO DRINK TOILET WATER?

Number one and number two

TOILET SEAT NAME GAME

Directions: Mrs. Master is a disaster! She helps A.J.'s class invent a heated, scented, talking, glow-in-the-dark toilet seat! What should they name it? Find twelve name ideas hidden in the jumble of letters below.

```
O X V E Y C U S H Y T U S H Y
A S R D O O T A M O U U T M N
W Q C L E Z V B U T T H U T R
L U L I L Y S U L A H O B U P
F A N N Y C A N N Y U T R R O
R T G G Q R H A R N N S A D O
A S L E G A C A S D D E T I P
P P B O N P T R A E E A L N O
L O M A G P R A I R R T B A M
A T N P L E G E N T T A D T A
N O T S I R F L U S H A L O T
C U F O H P W Y Z Q R N F R I
T A H P A R T Y P O O P E R C
B O N M J D F K S N N B O Y T
G L O W B O W L I E E S N D Z
```

cozy crapper   turdinator
cushy tushy
fanny canny   butt hut
hot seat   party pooper
thunder throne
squat spot   poopomatic
glow bowl   Sir Flushalot

MY WEIRDEST MATH PROBLEMS

A.J. hates math! Who needs math when we have calculators? But we bet you a million hundred dollars that you can't solve these math problems without one!

1. A.J. finds an old baseball card in his garage that is worth $10 million.* He decides to give $1 million each to Ryan, Michael, Alexia, and Neil. He's even going to give $1 million each to Andrea and Emily. How much money does he have left?

2. A.J. buys a volcano for $3. Ryan buys a tornado for $5. Michael buys a hurricane for $1.50. Neil buys an earthquake for $4.50. How much did these guys spend on natural disasters?

3. A.J. has a hole in his pants pocket. He puts $3 worth of coins into the pocket. Then 2 quarters, 3 dimes, a nickel, and 8 pennies fall out. How much money does A.J. have left?

4. A.J. sells his sister to Andrea for $5. Andrea sells her brother to A.J. for $3. How much money do A.J. and Andrea have now?

---

*The card is worth $10 million, not the garage!

OUT OF THIS WORLD CROSSWORD

Directions: See how well you know our solar system! Answer the questions on the next page to name these heavenly bodies.

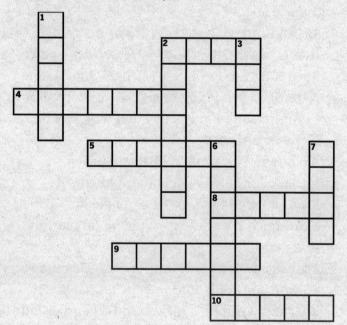

Across

2. Known as the red planet
4. The biggest planet in our solar system
5. A beautiful planet with rings
8. This used to be a planet but isn't anymore.
9. This planet has twenty-seven known moons.
   (Hint: A.J. played this in the class play.)
10. The planet we live on

Down

1. The hottest planet in our solar system
2. The smallest planet, closest to the sun
3. The center of our solar system
6. The coldest planet, farthest from the sun
7. It revolves around the earth.

DRAW AND COLOR LIKE CRAZY!

Call an ambulance! All the color has gone out of Ryan's face! Quick, grab some pencils or crayons before it's too late! Draw Ryan in the empty box below. Then color in the cover on the right. Hurry up!

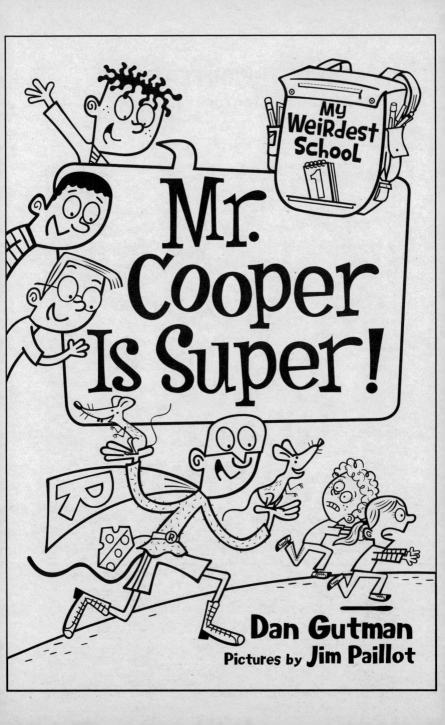

MY WEIRDEST SCHOOL

1

Mr. Cooper Is Super!

Dan Gutman

Pictures by Jim Paillot

SPOT THE DIFFERENCES

Directions: These two covers are almost identical. But there are a few differences. Can you spot them? (Hint: There are six.)

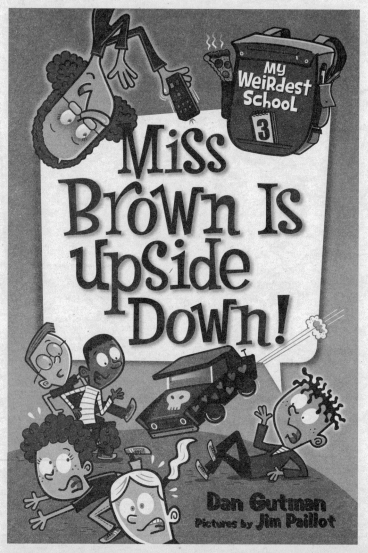

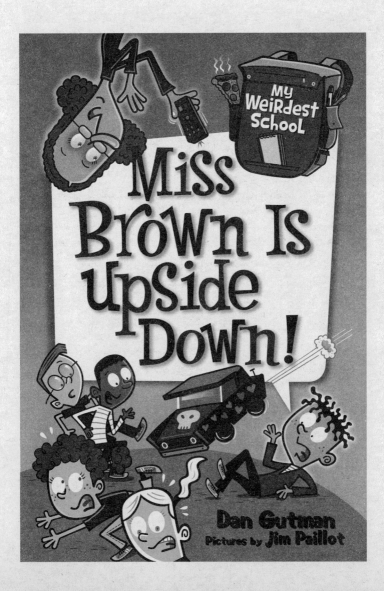

My WeiRdest School

Miss Brown Is Upside Down!

Dan Gutman

Pictures by Jim Paillot

WACKY WORD STORY TIME

Directions: Before you read this story, fill in each blank with a word that fits the description next to it. After you've filled in all the blanks, go back and read the story out loud. Is it funny? Or just really weird?

It's about time I get a turn! I was afraid that A.J. was going to hog the whole book.

My name is Andrea and I love _____ (*plural noun*) and _____ (*plural noun*) and _____ (*plural noun*) and _____ (*plural noun*) and all the stuff that A.J. says he hates.

The thing I like more than anything in the world is school. Going to school is fun. I like to learn new things. Like in language arts we learned the difference between a noun and a _____ (*animal*). In social studies we learned that America was named after a _____ (*noun*). In math we learned how to add and subtract _____ (*plural noun*). All these things are important to know so we will be able to grow up and go to _____ (*place*) someday.*

―――――――――――――――

*Hi! Thanks for looking down here. This is called a footnote. It's a note at the bottom of the page that explains

Ella Mentry School is so great because of our teachers. In second grade we had Miss Daisy. She was really nice, even though she liked to sit on a _____ (*noun*) and eat _____ (*plural noun*) all day. Then she got married to our reading specialist, Mr. Macky. They had a baby girl named Jackie Macky. She was really cute. Jackie couldn't do much, but she liked to put a _____ (*noun*) in her mouth all day.

When Miss Daisy left school to take care of Jackie, we moved up to third grade and got a new teacher named Mr. Granite. He was nice too. Mr. Granite was born on a _____ (*noun*) in a different galaxy. He came to Earth in a flying _____ (*noun*). One day a (*noun*) landed outside in the _____ (*noun*), so Mr. Granite had to leave us and go back to his home _____ (*noun*). That was sad.

After that Mr. Cooper became our teacher. I like him too. He wears a _____ (*noun*), and he thinks he is a _____ (*noun*). But he's not a very good one, because he's always tripping over a _____ (*noun*) and crashing into _____ (*plural noun*). One day Mr. Cooper

_____

something that was above. See? I just explained what a footnote is in the footnote! Okay, you can look up now. Bye!

was sick, so he had to go to _____ (*place*). And you'll never believe who our substitute teacher was that day. It was Miss Daisy! She came back! It's all part of the circle of life, I guess.

Let's see, what else can I tell you about me? I like to take classes after school and learn new things, like how to _____ (*verb*) a _____ (*noun*) and _____ (*verb*) a _____ (*noun*). I love music too. I'm a good singer, and I'm learning how to play a _____ (*noun*). I want to go to Harvard someday and become a successful _____ (*noun*).

Well, that's about it. I hope you enjoyed this little _____ (*noun*). Let me give you some _____ (*plural noun*) so you will become a better _____ (*noun*). Remember to read lots of _____ (*plural noun*), get _____ (*number*) hours of sleep every night, eat plenty of _____ (*plural noun*), and if you go outside in the summer, always put _____ (*noun*) on your skin.

Bye!

MY WEIRDEST SCHOOL TRIVIA

There's no way in a million hundred years you'll get all these answers right. So nah-nah-nah boo-boo on you! (Hint: All the answers to the questions below come from the My Weirdest School series.)

Q: WHAT ARE MR. GRANITE'S LAST WORDS AS HE FLIES AWAY IN A SPACESHIP?

A: "Turn to page twenty-three in your math books. . . ."

Q: WHAT IS MR. COOPER'S SUPERPOWER?

A: He can make you think of anything he wants you to think about.

Q: WHY DOES MR. GRANITE COME BACK TO ELLA MENTRY SCHOOL IN HIS SPACESHIP?

A: To return his key to the teachers' lounge

Q: HOW MUCH MONEY DOES ELLA MENTRY GIVE TO THE SCHOOL?

A: One million dollars

Q: WHAT IS THE NAME OF THE NEWS ANCHOR FOR DIRK SCHOOL?

A: Morgan Brocklebank

Q: HOW DOES MISS BROWN FIRST WALK INTO A.J.'S CLASSROOM?

A: On her hands, upside down

123

Q: MR. COOPER IS A SUPERHERO FROM WHERE?

A: The East Pole

Q: HOW DOES MRS. MEYER TURN OFF THE BEEPING SMOKE DETECTOR?

A: She smashes it to pieces with a fire extinguisher.

Q: WHAT IS THE ONE THING MISS DAISY KNOWS A LOT ABOUT?

A: Bonbons

Q: WHAT SONG DOES MRS. COONEY ALWAYS SING WHILE SHE WASHES HER HANDS?

A: "Zip-A-Dee-Doo-Dah"

Q: WHO SPONSORS THE BRAIN GAMES?
A: The Jiggly Gelatin Company

Q: WHAT DOES DIRK SCHOOL NAME THE CAR THEY BUILT FOR THE BRAIN GAMES?
A: The Dirk Mobile

Q: WHAT DOES MISS DAISY DO TO PROTECT HERSELF FROM GERMS?
A: She wears a hazmat suit.

Q: WHO INVENTED KITTY LITTER?
A: Ed Lowe

Q: WHAT IS MISS MOON'S FULL NAME?
A: Moonbeam Starlight

Q: WHAT DOES MS. LAGRANGE'S SUB, MISS JULIA, SERVE THE KIDS FOR LUNCH?
A: Water soup

Q: WHY DOES EMILY WEAR A SKI MASK ON PICTURE DAY?
A: She has a pimple.

Q: WHAT IS A.J.'S SUPERMODEL NAME?
A: Fabulo

Q: WHAT IS A.J.'S GRANDFATHER'S NAME?
A: Grandpa Bert

Q: WHAT DOES MRS. MASTER RIDE AROUND ON?
A: A hoverboard lawn mower

Q: HOW MUCH DOES THE CLASS DECIDE TO SELL THE PARTY POOPER FOR?
A: $99.99

Q: WHAT PLANET DOES A.J. GET PICKED TO BE IN THE CLASS PLAY?
A: Uranus

PART 5

VALENTINE HINK PINKS

Directions: Fill in the blanks based on the clues below. The answers to Hink Pinks are two rhyming words of one syllable each. To help you get the hang of it, we answered the first one for you!

I. CHOCOLATES FOR YOUR VALENTINE:
<u>SWEET</u> <u>TREAT</u>

2. INTELLIGENT BLOOD-PUMPING ORGAN:
_____ _____

3. ROAD MADE OF CANDY:
_____ _____

4. VALENTINE-SHAPED PICTURE:
_____ _____

5. AFFECTIONATE MITTEN:
_____ _____

6. VALENTINE-SHAPED BAKED GOOD:
_____ _____

HAPPY HOLIDAYS!

Directions: Here are ten holidays we celebrate in America. Fill in the months in which they occur.

1. HALLOWEEN _____

2. NEW YEAR'S DAY _____

3. CHRISTMAS _____

4. MEMORIAL DAY _____

5. KWANZAA _____

6. EASTER _____

7. PRESIDENTS' DAY _____

8. INDEPENDENCE DAY _____

9. THANKSGIVING _____

10. LABOR DAY _____

TRICK OR TREAT

Directions: Halloween is the coolest holiday because we get free candy. The person who thought up *that* idea should get the Nobel Prize.* Hidden in the jumble of letters below are fifteen candy names. Can you find them all?

```
O S V E Y S K I T T L E S Y M
A H R D O L T A M D U U T G I
W I C L E S V X N O T T P U L
L L A F F Y T A F F Y T B L K
H K L A T P U F S S E E R W D
G U M D R O P S N I R R A Y U
U M O N G K C A I E F F T O D
M S N E S T L E C R U N C H S
M E D R M T R A K I T K A T S
I D J D A A G E E L G A D P T
B C O S R S T A R B U R S T X
E U Y J T P S A S Y R U W H D
A A H O I S C E Y B A R T I O
R O N J E L L Y B E A N S Y T
S F L R S T W I Z Z L E R S S
```

Twizzlers   jelly beans
gumdrops   Nestlé Crunch
Almond Joy   Starburst
Skittles   Laffy Taffy
Smarties   gummi bears   Nerds
Milk Duds   Kit Kat   Snickers
Dots

*That's a prize for people who don't have bells.

130

OOH LA LA!

The new foreign exchange student, Pierre, is from France. Can you match these French facts to their correct answers below?

I. THE _____ WAS A GIFT FROM FRANCE TO THE UNITED STATES.

2. FRANCE IS ABOUT THE SAME SIZE AS _____ .

3. IN FRANCE THEY EAT _____ AND _____ .

4. THE _____ , _____ , AND _____ WERE ALL INVENTED IN FRANCE.

5. A FAMOUS BUILDING IN FRANCE IS THE _____ .

6. IN FRANCE, FRENCH FRIES ARE CALLED _____ .

Eiffel Tower   hot-air balloon
snails   Texas   Statue of Liberty
parachute   submarine
pommes frites   frogs' legs

HO! HO! HO!

Directions: Use this secret code to swap in letters below and find out what jobs these Ella Mentry School teachers do at the mall at Christmastime.

A B C D E F G H I J K L M
Z N E B H R K A U I F C W

N O P Q R S T U V W X Y Z
O L J D Q V P Y X G S M T

1. Mrs. Kormel

__ __ __ __   __ __ __   __ __ __ __ __
F I B X   Z E C   Z F H J B

__ __ __ __
F J Q C

2. Miss Lazar

__ __ __ __ __ __   __ __ __   __ __ __ __ __ __ __
K F N X Z U   Z E C   X B N M Y H B

3. Mrs. Roopy and Miss Holly
,

__ __ __ __ __ __   __ __ __ __ __ __
X H B Z H X   E C O T C F

__ __ __ __ __
C O S C X

4. Mr. Klutz

__ __ __ __ __   __ __ __ __ __
X H B Z H   L O H I X

WHAT IS ANDREA'S PROBLEM?

Directions: Andrea always lines up her stuff because she thinks being organized is really important. What is her problem? Now it's *your* problem. Help Andrea line up her school supplies in alphabetical order.

ALPHABETICAL ORDER:

crayons

calculator

notebook

hole punch

scissors

ruler

tape

glitter glue

stickers

Post-it notes

pens

glue stick

backpack

pencils

stapler

1. _____

2. _____

3. _____

4. _____

5. _____

6. _____

7. _____

8. _____

9. _____

10. _____

11. _____

12. _____

13. _____

14. _____

15. _____

CAMP OCKATOLLYQUAY

Directions: Summer's almost over. A.J., Andrea, and the gang are going to back-to-school day camp. Answer the questions below using only the letters in:

CAMP OCKATOLLYQUAY

I. A PERSON WHO IMITATES EVERYTHING

_____

2. THE SOUND A CHICKEN MAKES

_____

3. MESSY OR DISGUSTING _____

4. A KIND OF POWDER _____

5. ANIMAL THAT RHYMES WITH "MAMA"

_____

6. SOMETHING THAT TELLS TIME

_____

7. THE SOUND A DUCK MAKES _____

8. THE BIRD IN A CLOCK _____

CLOTHES SHOPPING SCRAMBLE

Directions: A.J. and Andrea are going to the mall to do some back-to-school clothes shopping. Is there anything more boring? Unscramble the letters below to find out what Andrea bought.

1. KROTS _____

2. ETHAPLER ASPTN _____ _____

3. GIGSNGEJ _____

4. DRIFGEN CORP POT _____ _____

   _____

5. WINOBAR SEDRS _____ _____

6. ZYZFU REUPS _____ _____

7. WOFLY KRITS _____ _____

ODE TO PEEPS

Directions: A.J. and his friends sure love Peeps! Fill in the missing words in their odes to Peeps below. (Hint: The *real* answers are in *My Weird School Special: Oh, Valentine, We've Lost Our Minds!* But feel free to improvise with your own.)

MICHAEL: I COULD EAT _____ OF PEEPS.

NEIL: I COULD EAT PEEPS IN MY _____ .

ALEXIA: ONLY _____ DON'T LIKE PEEPS.

RYAN: I _____ IF I DON'T GET PEEPS.

A.J.: I WISH I WAS _____-_____ IN PEEPS.

ANDREA: I WOULD _____ OVER _____ FOR PEEPS.

sleep knee weep sheep creeps heaps
leap deep

CHRISTMAS PRESENTS
WORD SEARCH

Directions: Can you find twelve presents A.J. wants for Christmas hidden in the jumble of letters below?

```
W S V E Y P O P H T B C A J Y
A N S D O L F A M S U L D M N
G I T L E S O X N L T A I I R
L C R I S C O O T E R T R L Z
F K I A T I T F Y D E P T K T
R S K A T E B O A R D R B Y V
I R E E G K A F S E F F I W I
S S R O N A L R A R I P K A D
B A S E B A L L G L O V E Y E
E D M F L A G E N L G A D P O
E V I N D D R O N E E Q S V G
C U T J A P T A B P T U H F A
T A H O C K E Y S T I C K I M
B O N M J D F K S U D B O Y E
C B U N X H E A D P H O N E S
```

skateboard football
video games
hockey stick
Striker Smith dirt bike
baseball glove headphones
sled scooter Frisbee
drone

137

A.J.'S HOLIDAY JOKES

Did you know that April 4 is World Rat Day?
And April 23 is International Nose-Picking Day.
National Talk in an Elevator Day is the last
Friday in July. Hey, we didn't make those up.
They're *real* holidays! Go ahead and look 'em up.
But first, enjoy these holiday jokes. . . .

WHAT NATIONALITY IS SANTA?
North Polish

WHAT IS SANTA'S FAVORITE SANDWICH?
Peanut butter and jolly

**WHAT DO YOU GET WHEN YOU CROSS A BELL
WITH A SKUNK?**
Jingle smells

WHY DOES SANTA HAVE A GARDEN?
So he can hoe-hoe-hoe.

**WHAT DO YOU CALL A VERY SMALL
VALENTINE?**
A Valentiny

**WHAT KIND OF FLOWERS SHOULD YOU
NEVER GIVE ON VALENTINE'S DAY?**
Cauliflowers

WHERE DOES THE EASTER BUNNY EAT BREAKFAST?

At IHOP

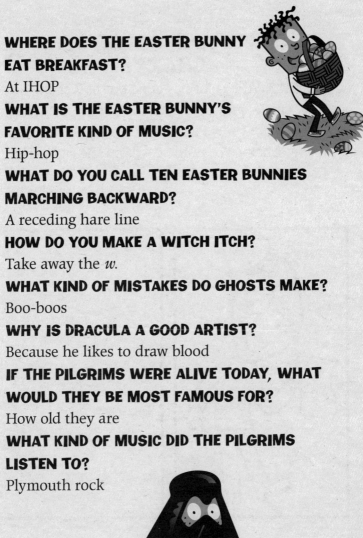

WHAT IS THE EASTER BUNNY'S FAVORITE KIND OF MUSIC?

Hip-hop

WHAT DO YOU CALL TEN EASTER BUNNIES MARCHING BACKWARD?

A receding hare line

HOW DO YOU MAKE A WITCH ITCH?

Take away the *w.*

WHAT KIND OF MISTAKES DO GHOSTS MAKE?

Boo-boos

WHY IS DRACULA A GOOD ARTIST?

Because he likes to draw blood

IF THE PILGRIMS WERE ALIVE TODAY, WHAT WOULD THEY BE MOST FAMOUS FOR?

How old they are

WHAT KIND OF MUSIC DID THE PILGRIMS LISTEN TO?

Plymouth rock

DRAW AND COLOR LIKE CRAZY!

Uh-oh! All the color has gone out of Pierre's face! Quick, grab some pencils or crayons before it's too late! Draw Pierre* in the empty box below. Then color in the cover on the right. The fate of France is in your hands!

---

*Also known as Pee-Air

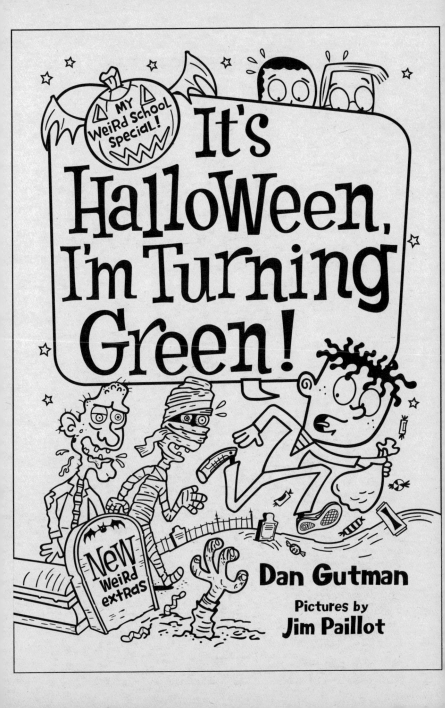

MY WeiRd School SpeciaL!

It's HalloWeen, I'm Turning Green!

NeW WeiRd extRas

Dan Gutman

Pictures by
Jim Paillot

SPOT THE DIFFERENCES

Directions: These two covers are almost identical. But there are a few differences. Can you spot them? (Hint: There are six.)

Dan Gutman

MY WeiRd SchooL SpeciaL!

Bunny Double We're In Trouble!

EXTRAS
GaMeS! PuzzLeS!
aND MoRe!

Pictures by
Jim Paillot

WACKY WORD STORY TIME

Directions: Before you read this story, fill in each blank with a word that fits the description next to it. After you've filled in all the blanks, go back and read the story out loud. Is it funny? Or just really weird?

My name is A.J. and I hate holidays.

Holidays are no fun. Do you want to know why? Well, first of all, you have to get dressed up. My mom always makes me wear a _____ (*noun*). I hate wearing a _____ (*same as previous word*)! She also makes me wear a _____ (*noun*) around my neck. Ugh! What's the point of that? I feel like I'm getting strangled! Whoever dreamed up that idea should have his _____ (*noun*) examined.

Then, once I'm all dressed up in my fancy _____ (*noun*), I have to sit in a _____ (*noun*) and drive a million hundred miles to my _____ (*type of female relative*)'s house. I love my _____ (*same as previous word*), but why does she have to live so far away? Couldn't she find a _____ (*noun*) that was closer to our _____ (*noun*)?

Once we get there, we have to eat. Eating is a big part of holidays, and you have to sit at the _____ (*noun*) for hours. And instead of eating stuff I like _____ (*noun*), _____ (*noun*), and _____ (*noun*), I have to eat weird, yucky foods like _____ (*noun*) and _____ (*noun*). One time I had to eat a _____ (*noun*). Ugh, gross! Can you believe that? Did you ever eat a _____ (*same as previous word*)? Believe me, it tastes horrible. I'd rather eat a _____(*noun*).

Oh, and we aren't allowed to watch TV during the holiday. No, we have to sit around for hours listening to the grown-ups talk about _____ (*plural noun*). Why do grown-ups talk about _____ (*same as previous word*) so much? What is their problem? I hope I never get to be a _____ (*noun*).

Finally, after the torture—I mean the holiday—is over, then I have to sit in the _____ (*noun*) and drive a million hundred miles home again. What a waste of gas!

That's why I hate holidays.

Well, my name is Andrea and I *love* holidays!

Getting dressed up is so much fun. I love to go into my closet and pick out my favorite _____ (noun). Then I put it on. I like to wear _____ (plural noun), _____ (plural noun), and _____ (plural noun). And it's fun to put a _____ (noun) on your head or wrap a _____ (noun) around your neck. Dressing up makes me feel like a real _____ (noun).

I'll tell you about the holiday that I hate the most. It's _____ (noun) Day. Isn't that ridiculous? They actually have a holiday to celebrate _____ (same as previous word). Who came up with *that* dumb idea? They should take that guy and put him in a _____ (noun).

If you ask me, I think we should get rid of all the weird holidays we have now and start all over again with some new holidays. For instance, we should have _____ (noun) Day. It would be a holiday to celebrate everything to do with _____ (plural of previous word). That would be cool. Here's how it would work. . . .

On the first Wednesday of _____ (noun), all the _____ (plural noun) and _____ (plural noun) would gather around a big _____ (noun) and sing a song about _____ (plural noun).

Then we would start throwing _____ (*plural noun*) at each other until we ran out of _____ (*same as previous word*). After that we would have to clean ourselves off by rubbing _____ (*plural noun*) all over our bodies. When all that is finished, we would go to the _____ (*noun*) and eat _____ (*plural noun*) until our_____ (*plural noun*) were about to burst. Now *that* would make a cool holiday!

A.J. didn't mention _____ (*noun*) Day, of course. That's my favorite holiday. On _____ (*same as previous word*) Day, you get to have a _____ (*noun*), and everybody gets to bring home a _____ (*noun*) with them. Then we eat them. Yum! That's why I love holidays so much.

MY WEIRD SCHOOL SPECIALS TRIVIA

There's no way in a million hundred years you'll get all these answers right. So nah-nah-nah boo-boo on you! (Hint: All the answers to the questions below come from the My Weird School Specials series.)

Q: WHAT DOES PIERRE DO WHEN HE MEETS EACH GIRL IN THE CLASS?

A: Kisses her hand

Q: WHAT GIFT DOES PIERRE BRING THE CLASS?

A: Cheese and crackers

Q: WHAT SONG DID PIERRE TEACH THE CLASS?

A: "Frère Jacques"

Q: WHERE DO PIERRE AND ANDREA GO ON THEIR DATE?

A: The I Scream Shop

Q: WHAT WAS A.J.'S SECRET PLAN FOR MISCHIEF NIGHT?

A: To soap Andrea's windows

Q: WHAT IS THE NAME OF MRS. YONKERS'S MICROWAVE INVENTION?

A: MicroMole 4000 Expandinator

Q: WHAT STREET NEVER HAS ANY GOOD CANDY ON HALLOWEEN?

A: Evergreen Avenue

Q: WHAT DOES ANDREA INTEND TO DO WITH HER HALLOWEEN CANDY?

A: Give it to poor people

Q: WHO DRIVES A.J. AND HIS FRIENDS TO THE MALL TO MEET SANTA?

A: Ryan's mom

Q: WHO IS THE MALL SECURITY GUARD AT CHRISTMASTIME?

A: Officer Spence

Q: WHO IS A.J.'S MOM'S BEST FRIEND?

A: Andrea's mom

Q: HOW MANY TIMES A DAY DOES ANDREA BRUSH HER TEETH?

A: Seven

Q: WHERE DID ANDREA'S MOTHER GO TO COLLEGE?

A: Harvard

Q: WHAT IS THE NAME OF THE PEN SPECIALIST AT STAPLES?

A: Mr. Debakey

Q: WHERE DOES A.J. SLEEP IN ANDREA'S BEDROOM?

A: On the floor

Q: WHAT IS THE NAME OF MAYOR HUBBLE'S HOUSE?

A: Hubble Manor

Q: HOW MANY BATHROOMS ARE IN MAYOR HUBBLE'S HOUSE?

A: Twenty-three

Q: WHAT IS THE NAME OF MAYOR HUBBLE'S WIFE?

A: Bubbles Hubble

Q: WHO IS INSIDE THE EASTER BUNNY COSTUME AT MAYOR HUBBLE'S PARTY?

A: Boomer Wiggins

Q: WHAT IS THE RAPPER CRAY-Z'S REAL NAME?

A: Johnny Cray

Q: WHAT CHRISTMAS SONG IS STUCK IN A.J.'S HEAD?

A: "The Christmas Klepto"

Q: WHAT NAME DOES NEIL CALL CRAY-Z?

A: Justin Timberlake

ANSWERS

WHO TEACHES WHAT?

Miss Daisy – **second grade**
Miss Holly – **Spanish**
Mr. Macky – **reading**
Ms. Hannah – **art**
Miss Small – **gym**
Mr. Hynde – **music**
Mrs. Yonkers – **computer skills**
Mr. Docker – **science**

ART SUPPLY SCRAMBLE

1. FINGER PAINT
2. GLUE STICKS
3. GLITTER
4. CARDBOARD
5. SCISSORS
6. NEWSPAPERS
7. CRAYONS
8. PAINTBRUSHES

FIZZ ED!

JUGGLE SCARVES
BALANCE FEATHERS
CHICKEN DANCE
Bonus: FUN, FUN, FUN ALL THE TIME!

A.J.'S SUDOKU FUN

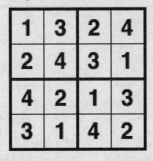

1	3	2	4
2	4	3	1
4	2	1	3
3	1	4	2

CHOCOLATE PARTY WORD SEARCH

MISS DAISY IS CRAZY!

$8 + 6 = \mathbf{14}$	$65 + 3 + 7 = \mathbf{75}$
$7 + 5 = \mathbf{12}$	$38 + 2 + 2 = \mathbf{42}$
$41 + 9 = \mathbf{50}$	$52 + 3 - 9 = \mathbf{46}$
$5 + 74 = \mathbf{79}$	$9 + 28 - 3 = \mathbf{34}$

TEACHERS IN LOVE MAZE

NURSERY RHYME WEEK

1. Jack and Jill
2. Little Miss Muffet
3. Humpty Dumpty
4. Little Bo Peep
5. Wee Willie Winkie
6. Georgie Porgie
7. Peter Peter Pumpkin Eater
8. Simple Simon

RAPPIN' AND RHYMIN' WITH MR. HYNDE

When I'm rappin', I need a beat.
And when I'm hungry, I like to **eat**.
When I'm thirsty, I take a drink.
Then I wash the dishes in the **sink**.
When I'm down, I'm feeling blue.
Pigs will squeal and cows will **moo**.
Some days when I'm not in school,
I go swimming in a **pool**.
To feed my brain, I read a book.
To feed my belly, I like to **cook**.
To make an egg, I always boil it.
When I gotta go, I use the **toilet**.
When I'm tired, I take a nap.
But mostly I just like to **rap**.

WHO'S WHO?

Mr. Klutz – **principal**
Mrs. Roopy – **librarian**
Mrs. Cooney – **school nurse**
Ms. LaGrange – **lunch lady**
Miss Lazar – **custodian**
Mrs. Kormel – **bus driver**
Mrs. Patty – **secretary**
Mr. Macky – **reading specialist**
Mr. Louie – **crossing guard**

SAY GOOD-BYE TO SUGAR!

1. CHEESE STICK
2. RAISINS
3. ORANGE
4. APPLE
5. YOGURT
6. GRAPES
7. CARROTS
8. PEANUTS

MUSICAL MAYHEM

SPORTS SEARCH

THROWING UP ON THE ROOF!

1. UMBRELLA
2. FOOTBALL
3. BASEBALL CAP
4. NOTEBOOK
5. YOYO
6. FRISBEE
7. TENNIS RACKET

FUN WITH POTATOES!

1. A popular Mexican food – **taco**
2. A type of large parrot – **cockatoo**
3. Chocolaty hot drink – **cocoa**
4. A lively type of dance – **polka**
5. Popular soda flavor – **cola**
6. Another word for "cape" – **cloak**
7. To applaud – **clap**
8. Complete or absolute – **total**

MRS. KORMEL IS NOT NORMAL!

1. Bingle boo – **Hello**
2. Limpus kidoodle – **Sit down**
3. Zingy zip – **Quiet down**
4. Bix blattinger – **curse word**
5. Pinkle burfle nobin – **Get off the bus**

MASHED POTATO MESSAGE

YOU ARE WHAT YOU EAT
Bonus: GIVE PEAS A CHANCE

PRESIDENTIAL TRUE OR FALSE

1. Franklin Roosevelt's mother made him wear dresses until he was five. **T**
2. Abraham Lincoln had wooden teeth. **F**
3. Ulysses S. Grant smoked twenty cigars a day. **T**
4. Andrew Johnson never went to school. **T**
5. Thomas Jefferson grew some of the first tomatoes in America. **T**
6. John Quincy Adams liked to go skinny-dipping. **T**
7. Benjamin Franklin was our third president. **F**

SPOT THE DIFFERENCES

FUN IN THE SUN CROSSWORD

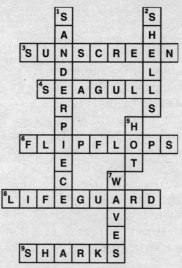

HINKY PINKIES

1. Glove for a baby cat – **kitten mitten**
2. Miss Daisy's baby –**Jackie Macky**
3. Rocky celestial body –**granite planet**
4. Bizarre flower – **crazy daisy**
5. Happy Christmas shrub – **jolly holly**
6. Cheerful joke – **sunny funny**
7. Coach Hyatt's son – **Wyatt Hyatt**

JAIL JUMBLE

1. SLAMMER
2. CALABOOSE
3. COOLER
4. CLINK
5. JOINT
6. POKEY
7. HOOSEGOW

TEAM SPIRIT CHEERS

Jump in the air! Fall in the **dirt**!
Just make sure no one gets hurt!
Laugh and play and **shout** and sing!
Winning isn't everything!
Losing! Winning! We won't lie!
We're most happy with a **tie**!
We don't **hate** and we don't boo!
We respect the other team, too!
Football has a kicker. Baseball has a **batter**!
Whatever game we play, the score doesn't matter!
Winning! Losing! It depends!
Why can't we just all be **friends**?
That's all **right**! That's okay!
We're gonna win it anyway!
It's okay that we're not **great**!
At least we all participate!

PERFECT FOOD COMBOS

1. Peaches and **cream**
2. Fish and **chips**
3. Franks and **beans**
4. Bacon and **eggs**
5. Macaroni and **cheese**
6. Milk and **cookies**
7. Spaghetti and **meatballs**
8. Peas and **carrots**
9. Cheese and **crackers**
10. Burger and **fries**

TRUE OR FALSE?

1. Mrs. Lizzy is not a real teacher. **T**
2. Mr. Granite is from the planet Uranus. **F**
3. Ms. LaGrange is from Spain. **F**
4. Mrs. Roopy's hero is Melvil Dewey. **T**
5. There's a hot tub in the teachers' lounge. **F**
6. A.J. loves Mrs. Cooney. **T**
7. Miss Lazar loves when kids make messes. **T**
8. Mrs. Dole is Ryan's mom. **T**
9. Miss Mary is Mr. Klutz's daughter. **T**
10. Ms. Leakey opened a McDonald's restaurant. **F**

PRINCIPAL CAMP WORD SEARCH

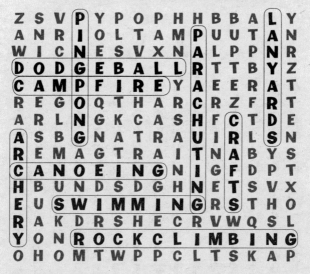

DR. BRAD'S DICTIONARY

zeez – **this**
shtop – **stop**
verd – **word**
furzer – **further**
uzzer – **other**
ees – **is**
zink – **think**
anuzer – **another**
eet – **it**
vy – **why**
zend – **send**
vill – **will**
verld – **world**
ven – **when**

WIN MONEY OR EAT BUGS!

162

FUN AT RECESS

1. How to make balloon animals
2. How to milk Pootie the goat
3. How to make a banjo out of toothpicks
4. How to yodel
5. How to play the ukulele
6. How to make armpit farts
7. Worm composting
8. How to ride a unicycle

MISS MARY'S RIDDLEGRAM

| ¹B | ²O | ³G | | ⁴S | ⁵N | ⁶O | ⁷R | ⁸K | ⁹E | ¹⁰L | ¹¹I | ¹²N | ¹³G |

A. SKIN
B. BOOGER
C. LONG

WHAT DO YOU LIKE ON YOUR PIZZA?

```
Z S V E Y P O P O T B B A J Y
A N P D O L P I N E A P P L E
W Z E L E S V X I O T T P A R
L A P R C B A L O N E Y B L Z
G I P A T I N F N S E E R O T
R E E G Q T C A S A L A M I Z
A V R E S K H A S M F F T X E
P T O M A T O S A U C E I C N
L P N A U T V A I S H N W H S
A I I F S A I E N H E A Q E T
M L U N A S E G H R V Q V E X
C U F J G P S I R O S U A S O
T A H E E S H E Y O E R A E L
B O N M J D F H A M D B S Y T
P E P P E R S U T S M P T I M
```

163

THE SECRET MATH LESSON

1. frustrated
2. indigestion
3. None. Miss Lazar, the custodian, screws in the lightbulbs.
4. all of them
5. I have no idea what you are talking about.

MR. SLUG'S SECRET CODE

I FEEL LOUSY. I AM SO TIRED.
I NEED TO LIE DOWN!

SPOT THE DIFFERENCES

THIS PLACE IS A ZOO!

ZOO ZONES

1. Lion **Lane**
2. Turtle **Town**
3. Alligator **Avenue**
4. Lizard **Lane**
5. Rhino **Road**
6. Bat **Boulevard**
7. Zebra **Zone**
8. Snake **Street**
9. Hedgehog **Highway**
10. Penguin **Paradise**

WHO'S WHO AT ELLA MENTRY SCHOOL?
1. Never ties his shoes – **Michael**
2. Will eat anything, even stuff that isn't food – **Ryan**
3. The nude kid – **Neil**
4. Crybaby – **Emily**
5. Little Miss Perfect – **Andrea**
6. Skateboarding tomboy – **Alexia**
7. Lives around the corner from A.J. – **Billy**
8. Is always picking his nose – **Wyatt**
9. A.J.'s sister – **Amy**
10. Hates school – **A.J.**

MR. FIX-IT WORD SCRAMBLE
1. COFFEE MACHINE
2. COMPUTER
3. LASER PRINTER
4. INTERCOM
5. PENCIL SHARPENER
6. MICROPHONE
7. COPY MACHINE
8. SMART BOARD

FAKE NEWS
1. MS. COCO IS A CAR THIEF!! **A**
2. MR. KLUTZ HAS TWO WIVES!! **D**
3. MRS. YONKERS SETS FIRES FOR FUN!! **B**
4. MR. MACKY SPOTTED KISSING MARRIED WOMAN!! **C**
5. OFFICER SPENCE WAS IN JAIL FOR FIVE YEARS!! **E**

ELEVEN TIMES ELEVEN TABLE

11 x 1 = **11**	11 x 7 = **77**
11 x 2 = **22**	11 x 8 = **88**
11 x 3 = **33**	11 x 9 = **99**
11 x 4 = **44**	11 x 10 = **110**
11 x 5 = **55**	11 x 11 = **121**
11 x 6 = **66**	

YEE-HA!

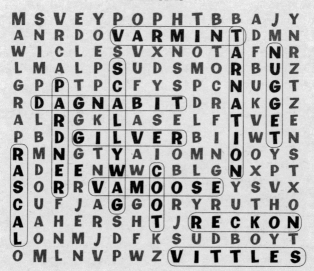

SAVE MISS KRAFT'S LIFE!

1. Alabama
2. Alaska
3. Arizona
4. Arkansas
5. California
6. Colorado
7. Connecticut
8. Delaware
9. Florida
10. Georgia
11. Hawaii
12. Idaho
13. Illinois
14. Indiana
15. Iowa
16. Kansas
17. Kentucky
18. Louisiana
19. Maine
20. Maryland
21. Massachusetts
22. Michigan
23. Minnesota
24. Mississippi
25. Missouri
26. Montana
27. Nebraska
28. Nevada
29. New Hampshire
30. New Jersey
31. New Mexico
32. New York
33. North Carolina
34. North Dakota
35. Ohio
36. Oklahoma
37. Oregon
38. Pennsylvania
39. Rhode Island
40. South Carolina
41. South Dakota
42. Tennessee
43. Texas
44. Utah
45. Vermont
46. Virginia
47. Washington
48. West Virginia
49. Wisconsin
50. Wyoming

WHAT IS A.J.'S FAVORITE SUBJECT?

GEDNIRA **(R)E A D I N G**

ICESNCE **S C I E N C (E)**

HAMTATECISM **M A T H E M A T I (C) S**

ZIZF DE **F I Z Z (E) D**

OILCAS SUITEDS **(S) O C I A L**
S T U D I E (S)

Answer: **RECESS**

AJ'S CAMPAIGN PROMISES

1. Abolish homework. **Y**
2. Kids will wear school uniforms. **N**
3. Every day will be a snow day. **Y**
4. There will be fewer fire drills. **N**
5. Abolish anything higher than the five times table. **Y**
6. Teachers will be replaced by comic book superheroes. **Y**
7. Water fountains will be filled with lemonade. **N**
8. A video game system will be built into every desk. **Y**

DR. NICHOLAS'S RIDICULOUS CROSSWORD PUZZLE

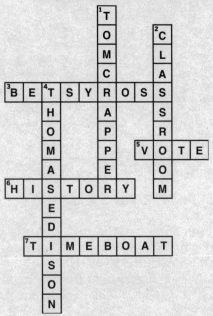

MY WEIRD DOGS

1. Chihuahua + dachshund = chiweenie
2. schnauzer + Yorkie = snorkie
3. pappillon + poodle = papi-poo
4. dachshund + poodle = doxiepoo
5. collie + poodle = cadoodle
6. Chihuahua + pug = chug
7. schnauzer + poodle = schnoodle
8. bulldog + whippet = bullwhip

HOW TALENTED ARE YOU?

```
M S V E Y P O P H T B B A J Y
J N R D O N O S E F L U T E N
U Y O D E L I N G O X E P I R
G C M X L V D U L T A B L Z Z
G K A R M P I T F A R T S K J
L E G G Q T H A R P R I O Z O
I R I E G K C A S D F N T U K
N S C O N A T R A I G L F E E
G E T A G T R A I N B B L B S
B U R P I N G E N C I G D P T
M O I N D S D G H E G S S X O
C U C J A P B A B N R S T K L
T A K R A P P I N G A R T O T
B O S M J D F K S U D B O I T
L I P S Y N C H I N G S K S P
```

MANAGE YOUR MONEY

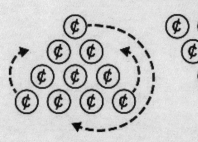

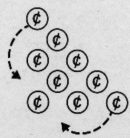
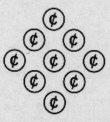

171

THE SECRET CARNIVAL CODE

TOILET SEAT TOSS
GOATING BOOTH
BIG CAR SMASH
COW PIE BINGO
KISS A TOAD

SPOT THE DIFFERENCES

A.J. AND ANDREA SITTING IN A TREE
IF THOSE GUYS WEREN'T MY BEST FRIENDS,
I WOULD HATE THEM!

MORE WHO'S WHO?
1. New third-grade teacher – **Mr. Cooper**
2. Digital media arts teacher – **Ms. Cuddy**
3. Brain Games coach – **Miss Brown**
4. Firefighter – **Mrs. Meyer**
5. Substitute teacher – **Miss Daisy**
6. New principal – **Mr. Nick**
7. School photographer – **Ms. Joni**
8. Alexia's grandmother/inventor – **Mrs. Master**
9. Miss Universe – **Miss Tracy**

PIZZA MATH
1. $12.50
2. 1 hour
3. Half, or 4 slices
4. 6 slices or $6/8$ths or $3/4$ths

WORLD WAR WEIRD!

	Ella Mentry	OR Dirk
1. Sings songs from *Annie*	X	___
2. Clog dances on top of news desk	X	___
3. Re-creates Michael Jackson's "Thriller" video	___	X
4. Puts parents on TV	X	___
5. Plays *Win Money or Eat Bugs!* reality show	___	X
6. Stages a zombie-and-vampire attack	X	___
7. Plays *Killer Karaoke* reality show	___	X

BRAIN GAMES CAR MAZE

ONLY YOU CAN PREVENT FOREST FIRES!

1. Liquid soap – **BODY WASH**
2. These are above your eyes on your face – **EYEBROWS**
3. To brag – **BOAST**
4. The planet we live on – **EARTH**
5. A type of shellfish – **OYSTER**
6. Kind of hat they wear in France – **BERET**
7. Something you use in sewing – **THREAD**

MRS. MEYER'S FIRE RULES

1. STOP, DROP, AND ROLL
2. FALL AND CRAWL
3. DON'T HIDE. GO OUTSIDE.

GERM WARFARE

1. DOORKNOBS
2. BABIES
3. TOILET SEATS
4. TELEPHONES
5. BABY TOYS
6. SNEAKERS
7. KITCHEN COUNTER
8. HANDS

WHAT'S WRONG WITH MR. COOPER?

A. IGNORANT
B. NEW
C. OIL

NO COFFEE!

```
T S V E Y P O P H T B B A J Y
A N R D O L C A M O U U C M N
S I C C R E A M E R T T U I R
U C M G H K P A I S T T P L Z
G K F R A P P U C C I N O K T
A E G O Q T U A R I R R F Y Z
R R L U D E C A F E F F J W B
P S B N N H C R A R I P O A E
L E M D G T I A I O N N E Y A
A D N S L A N E N L G A D P N
M B J D W M O C H A E J S V S
C R F J A P H A D T W A Z H O
T E S P R E S S O T A V T I L
D W N M C O F F E E M A K E R
O J U S E O R P Z N Y T C L O
```

LOVEY-DOVEY SCRAMBLE

1. ANGEL MUFFIN
2. SUGARPLUM
3. DARLING
4. SWEETHEART
5. HONEY BUN
6. SWEETIE PIE
7. SUGAR LIPS

WHAT DID RYAN WEAR ON PICTURE DAY?

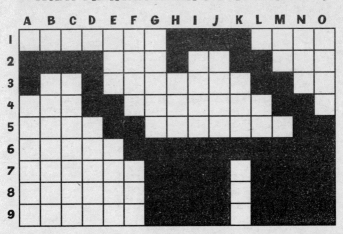

Answer: Sunglasses!

TOILET SEAT NAME GAME

```
O X V E Y C U S H Y T U S H Y
A S R D O O T A M O U U T M N
W Q C L E Z V B U T T H U T R
L U L I L Y S U L A H O B U P
F A N N Y C A N N Y U T R D O
R T G G Q R H A R N N S A I O
A S L E G A C A S D E E T N P
P P B O N P T R A E R A L A O
L O M A G P R A I R T T B T M
A T N P L E G E N T T A D O A
N O T S I R F L U S H A L O T
C U F O H P W Y Z Q R N F R I
T A H P A R T Y P O O P E R C
B O N M J D F K S N N B O Y T
G L O W B O W L I E E S N D Z
```

MY WEIRDEST MATH

1. $4 million
2. $14
3. $2.07
4. A.J. has $2 and Andrea has $3.

OUT OF THIS WORLD CROSSWORD

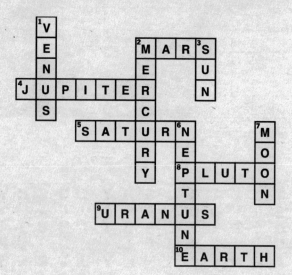

SPOT THE DIFFERENCES

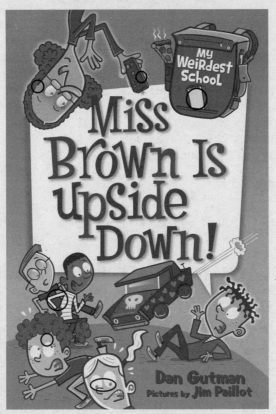

VALENTINE HINK PINKS

1. Chocolates for your valentine: **sweet treat**
2. Intelligent blood-pumping organ: **smart heart**
3. Road made of candy: **sweet street**
4. Valentine-shaped picture: **heart art**
5. Affectionate mitten: **love glove**
6. Valentine-shaped baked good: **heart tart**

HAPPY HOLIDAYS!

1. Halloween – **October**
2. New Year's Day – **January**
3. Christmas – **December**
4. Memorial Day – **May**
5. Kwanzaa – **December**
6. Easter – **April or sometimes March**
7. Presidents' Day – **February**
8. Independence Day – **July**
9. Thanksgiving – **November**
10. Labor Day – **September**

TRICK OR TREAT

OOH LA LA!

1. The **Statue of Liberty** was a gift from France to the United States.
2. France is about the same size as **Texas**.
3. In France they eat **snails** and **frogs' legs**.
4. The **parachute**, **submarine,** and **hot-air balloon** were all invented in France.
5. A famous building in France is the **Eiffel Tower**.
6. In France, french fries are called **pommes frites**.

HO! HO! HO!

1. Mrs. Kormel
   RUNS THE TRAIN RIDE
2. Miss Lazar
   FROSTY THE SNOWMAN
3. Mrs. Roopy and Miss Holly
   SANTA'S HELPER ELVES
4. Mr. Klutz
   SANTA CLAUS

WHAT IS ANDREA'S PROBLEM?

1. backpack
2. calculator
3. crayons
4. glitter glue
5. glue stick
6. hole punch
7. notebook
8. pencils
9. pens
10. Post-it notes
11. ruler
12. scissors
13. stapler
14. stickers
15. tape

CAMP OCKATOLLYQUAY

1. A person who imitates everything – **copycat**
2. The sound a chicken makes – **cluck**
3. Messy or disgusting – **yucky**
4. A kind of powder – **talcum**
5. Animal that rhymes with "mama" – **llama**
6. Something that tells time – **clock**
7. The sound a duck makes – **quack**
8. The bird in a clock – **cuckoo**

CLOTHES SHOPPING SCRAMBLE

1. SKORT
2. PLEATHER PANTS
3. JEGGINGS
4. FRINGED CROP TOP
5. RAINBOW DRESS
6. FUZZY PURSE
7. FLOWY SKIRT

ODE TO PEEPS

Michael: I could eat **heaps** of Peeps.
Neil: I could eat Peeps in my **sleep.**
Alexia: Only **creeps** don't like Peeps.
Ryan: I **weep** if I don't get Peeps.
A.J.: I wish I was **knee-deep** in Peeps.
Andrea: I would **leap** over **sheep** for Peeps.

CHRISTMAS PRESENTS WORD SEARCH

```
W S V E Y P O P H T B C A J Y
A N I S D O L F A M S U L D M I L Z
G I C T L E S O X N L T A T R I N R Z
L K K R I S C O O T E R A T R L K Y T
F R I I A T I T F Y D E P R B Y Y I
R S K A T E B O A R D R E I W Z D V
I R E E G K A F S E F F K A A E
S S R O N A L R A R I P Y O E
B A S E B A L L G L O V E D G A
E D M I F L A G E N L G A D P D R O N E E Q S V F M
E V U T N A D R O N E E Q S V F M
C U A I J A P T A B P T U H F A
T A H O C K E Y S T I C K I M
B O N M J D F K S U D B O Y E
C B U N X H E A D P H O N E S
```

SPOT THE DIFFERENCES

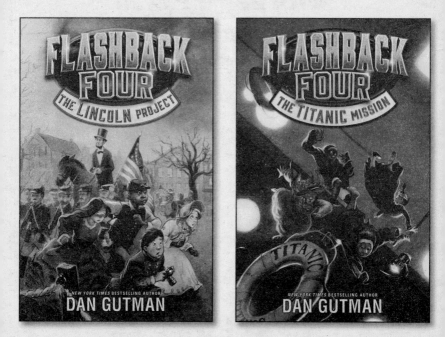

Rediscover Some of
BASEBALL'S GREATEST LEGENDS
with Dan Gutman

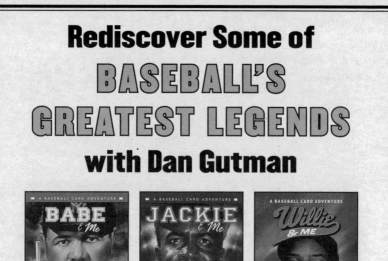

Joe Stoshack has the ability to travel back in time—using baseball cards as his time machine!

Follow Joe as he travels back to meet some of baseball's greatest sports heroes.